Bridging the Technology Gap

Bridging the Technology Gap
Historical Perspectives on Modern Asia

Printed in Seoul, Republic of Korea.

Seoul National University Press
1 Gwanak-ro, Gwanak-gu, Seoul 151-742, Republic of Korea.

E-mail : snubook@snu.ac.kr
Home-page: http://www.snupress.com

First Printing: Sept. 27, 2013

ISBN 978-89-521-1412-9 94910

Historical Research Series 01

Bridging the Technology GAP

Historical Perspectives on Modern Asia

Edited by Youngsoo Bae and Buhm Soon Park

SNUPRESS
Seoul National University Press

Preface

There remains a wide technology gap between nations, though some countries made a great progress in catching up with developed countries during the last decades. Many developing countries are left behind, while industrialized nations continue to mobilize people and resources toward technological progress. In addition, there is a serious gap within nations; people have different access to advanced technology, depending upon their region, income or generation.

These gaps have attracted attention among social scientists, along with policy makers, who are mainly concerned with technology diffusion since intellectual property rights are increasingly consolidated these days. Needless to say, however, technology diffusion is part of the larger process in which humankind has made advances in technology from time immemorial. Moreover, this process involves not merely economic development but cultural, social and political changes. Still, it is true that besides specialists in the history of science and technology, historians interested in the other fields have by and large neglected issues related to the technology gap.

Such a consideration led the Institute of Historical Research, Seoul National University, to hold an international conference in early November 2010. The conference, titled "Bridging the Technology Gap," asked historians in general, as well as specialists in the history of science and technology, to think about how developing countries understood the technology gap they had with advanced countries and the efforts they made to bridge it. Focusing on Asia since the late 19th century, it called attention to the broad context in which nations built up technological capabilities, such as educational reform, social movements, political initiatives, or other projects that they had launched trying to catch up with industrialized countries. In other words, the event was organized to encourage historians to provide historical perspectives to current discussion about the technology gap.

The international conference turned out to be a two-day-long warm conversation among responsive participants, including five Korean speakers and three international speakers from Australia, India and Singapore. By the closing session, speakers had begun talking about a book developing out of the conference. Two speakers were not able to follow up for personal reasons; instead an engineer who helped to design a nuclear power plant in Korea joined the ensuing process, making an eye-witness description of technological transfer beyond the national boundary. The end result is this handy book.

A number of people played an essential part in this final product as well as in the international conference. First of all, the contributors made the conference into this book by revising their paper. I feel heavily indebted to these friends, in particular Professors Low and Amir, who took a long trip to Seoul in November 2010. I would also like to sincerely thank Dr. Byung-Koo Kim for his generosity with manuscripts; he kindly allowed part of his autobiography to be reprinted in this book.

Thanks also goes to Professor Buhm Soon Park, who agreed to find time to review the whole manuscripts and write an introduction, while immersed in another project during his 2011-12 sabbatical. Furthermore, I am deeply appreciative of the prompt and appropriate advice offered by Professor Jong-tae Lim and other colleagues at the SNU Institute of Historical Research who helped to organize the international conference in November 2010. Special thanks to my meticulous editor Hyunho Kim, who paid attention to each and every detail of this book.

Youngsoo Bae
Professor of History, Seoul National University

Contents

Introduction*

Buhm Soon Park

Today, Korean companies often make headline news with their impressive performance in the global market. Samsung has emerged as the number one producer of smart phones, beating seemingly invincible giants like Apple and Nokia. Automobiles made by Hyundai, until recently known better for their affordable prices than for their high quality, have made their inroad into the market of both high-end and low-end classes. In the field of nuclear power plant construction, the Korea Electric Power Corporation (KEPCO, 한국전력공사) has led an international consortium to win a 40 billion dollar contract with the United Arab Emirates, sending a wake-up call to its big-name rivals, such as General Electric of America and Areva of France. For many policymakers in developing countries, Korea stands out as an attractive model of economic growth, transforming itself from a war-stricken, poor recipient of international aid into a world-leading seller of high-tech products. For

* Part of this introductory essay has been published in my article, "Rethinking the Technology Gap," *Korean Journal for the History of Science*, 33 (2011): 297-300.

the Japanese leaders, who have seen Sony, Toyota, Hitachi and Mitsubishi become household names in several industrial sectors for the past few decades, the urgent question now is how to maintain technological competitiveness and innovative sprit amidst the strong challenges from Korea, China, and other nations, which had studied the Japanese miracle in order to devise their catch-up strategies. The technology gap between Japan and some other Asian countries, as well as that between the West and the East, seems to have been significantly narrowed these days.

What made it possible for Asian countries to have such a turnaround in technology? A body of literature seeks to answer this question by examining cultural aspects (e.g., Asian values), innovation systems (e.g., government agencies and policies), geopolitical situations (e.g., the Cold War context), or charismatic leadership in business and policymaking areas (e.g., the founders of Sony and Samsung). Yet no one has taken a serious look into the nature of the technology gap per se. What is the technology gap? What exactly do we mean by "bridging" this gap? Is there a universal yardstick to measure and rank the national capacity for technological productivity? I think that the term 'gap' is a useful yet problematic metaphor, for a gap connotes a space or distance between two objects. Is the technology gap something that can be filled with more stuff or be connected with a bridge?

To better understand the meaning of the technology gap, we need to pay more attention to the ways in which technology is developed and used, namely the historicity of technology. Technology can be decontextualized from one place and be recontextualized in another, but the process is very complicated and is not easily accomplished. For example, building a factory for high-tech materials in India or China does not necessarily mean that technology is fully transferred and contextualized there. This is merely a change in the site of production. Andrew Feenberg, a philosopher of technology, maintains that the part can only be understood within the whole environment. A picture of an engine in a manufacture's catalog, with its sharp-edged surfaces in cold, shiny steel, is like an image of a fish out of water, giving no sense of the engine's noisy and hot working environment. Likewise, a study of the community or society is needed in order to understand how imported or transferred technology really works in the new environment.[1]

Nevertheless we tend to forget the contextualized or historicized meaning of technology. A good example is the inward-outward opening door, which is commonly seen in any movie theater. The invention of this type of swirling door is in fact an outcome of severe fire accidents that took place in theaters, including the famous Iroquois Theater fire in Chicago in 1903. Some 600 people died, and many of the victims were found near the exit door. Installation of inward-outward doors in theaters, then, became a construction standard, not an option. But very few people these days would be aware of this historical context behind door technology. Feenberg calls this "the paradox of origins," which means that "behind everything rational there lies a forgotten history."[2]

As a historian, I embrace Feenberg's emphasis on the historicity of technology. But I wonder how contextualized understanding of technol-

---

1 Andrew Feenberg, "Ten Paradoxes of Technology," *Technē* 14 (2010): 3-15. I am much inspired by Feenberg's critical view of technology, on which he gave a presentation at KAIST in 2010. See also Feenberg, *Between Reason and Experience: Essays in Technology and Modernity* (Cambridge, Mass., 2010).

2 Ibid.

ogy might help tackle the issue of the technology gap. Who cares about all the forgotten history when we are busy with catching-up? Do we have to learn all the trials and errors and study successes and failures before adopting and using technology? Technology can be liberated from its origin as much as it is constrained in the past. Let us take an example of the computer motherboard. One may find that the components of a motherboard are made in several different countries, assembled yet in another country, and sold all over the world. The motherboard is then an ensemble of patents protected, technologies transferred, labors purchased, and contracts signed. The same can be said of smart phones, automobiles, and nuclear power plants. The nationality of a technology becomes fuzzy, and the technology gap gets complicated, as it can be an issue of original inventions, manufacturing know-hows, management skills, or even business practices.

It should be noted, therefore, that the technology gap is not solely about technology itself. It is about the historical process by which technology moves beyond its birthplace, crosses national boundaries and business lines, and is put into a new use. This process often involves changes in government policies, corporate strategies, research directions, university teachings, and the way people live in society in general. The technology gap functions essentially as a rhetoric that sustains this historical process by constructing hopes and aspirations for progressive changes in developing countries.

The essays in this volume examine the historical processes of bridging the technology gap in three Asia countries—Japan, Indonesia, and Korea—in their unique sociopolitical contexts. To be sure, it may not be possible to generalize too much about the technology gap with these cases. Yet they can provide invaluable insight for understanding each country's experience of modernization of which technological leapfrogging was a key element.

Morris Low, for instance, contends that modernization in Japan was neither simply a process of westernization nor a rejection of the tradition. To him, it was a process of assimilating Western technology to Japanese culture. While the Meiji era (1868-1912) witnessed the influx of Western technological products and systems ranging from telegraphy and architecture to civil and mechanical engineering into Japan, the people there could adopt and further develop them without ever becoming Western. Low seeks to find the sources of this hybrid nature of Japanese technology, well expressed in the late nineteenth century slogan *wakon yōsai* ("Japanese spirit, Western technology"), particularly examining foreign teachers of engineering, who were instrumental in establishing and running educational institutions like Imperial College of Engineering. Those educators were the mediators between Western learning and Japanese tradition, or, to put it differently, the agents of decontextualizing technology from the West and recontextualizing it in Japan. Low sees that Japan's unique "technological culture" was also important in the reconstruction of the country after the end of World War II by rapidly catching up with the West, and yet he also raises an important question of whether it can help maintain Japan's leadership position in technology amidst the fierce international competition especially with Korea and China.

In terms of the means and goals of modernization, the Indonesian case is not much different from that of Japan. To close the gap in technology with the industrially advanced nations was perceived as the best way to modernization, while the goals were to achieve the independent and autonomous condition of governance, called mandiri. Sulfikar Amir provides a detailed account of the development and exercise of the state's developmental strategy in which high technology like aircraft manufacturing took an important place for accelerating socio-economic transformation of post-colonial Indonesia. Amir's focus is on the role of engineer-turned-technocrats, not economist-turned-technocrats, in formulating national policies for science and technology during the New Order regime (1966-1998). The political stability during this period allowed a small group of Europe-educated engineers to forge an alliance with those in power and plant their high-tech vision deep into the state's bureaucratic structure. The establishment of two government institutions, the Agency for the Assessment and Application of Technology (BPPT) and the Managing Agency for Strategic Industries (BPIS), was particularly significant for the technocrats to pursue technology-driven social changes, i.e., modernization through technology. Like in Japan, modernization in Indonesia did not simply mean westernization. Rather, it was the state's project wrapped in a nationalistic rhetoric and undertaken with a nationalistic fervor. The key technocrat, B. J. Habibie, later ascended to the highest political position in 1998 as the third President of Indonesia, succeeding his master and collaborator he had long served. Amir wonders, then, what kind of long-term effect the Asian economic crisis at that time would have upon the alliance of politics and science that had been seen as a successful marriage.

The rest of the volume deals with the Korean case in the second half of the twentieth century. Post-colonial Korea underwent drastic social and political changes after the end of World War II, which led to the establishment of two independent governments in the South and the North and subsequently to the bloody civil war between the two (1950-1953). The Korean peninsula became a showcase of the Cold War confrontations. Tae Gyun Park examines the development of science and technology in South Korea not from the perspective of inside-out but from that of outside-in. This does not mean, he has cautioned, that there was no internal drive for modernizing Korea with the upgraded scientific and technological capacities. Rather, his point is that the Cold War context, especially the influence of the U.S. foreign policies, has largely been set aside just as a large, political context. Park seeks to give a proper assessment of external factors, which could play a more decisive role than internal ones, at least in some key events. Such historical events include the educational reform of the South Korean universities after the 1945 liberation under the U.S. Army Military Government; the Minnesota Plan of the 1950s that sent a large number of faculty members at Seoul National University to the U.S. for advanced training in various academic fields; the 1966 establishment of the Korea Institute of Science and Technology spurred by the Johnson administration's foreign policy during the Vietnam War; and the take-off of Korean military industry after the announcement of the Nixon Doctrine that stressed the "Asianization" of regional defense issues. Park also points out the significance of the 1965 Korea-Japan normalization treaty, which made possible the flow of economic support and technological assistance from Japan. In emphasizing the U.S. role in shaping Korea's policy for science and technology, Park does not intend to argue that it was always positive and constructive. Rather, he also considers the constraints that the scientists and technocrats in Korea had felt extremely uncomfortable—to the extent that a group of scientists had left for the North before the Korean War.

While Tae Gyun Park seeks to broaden our scope to the Cold War international relations, Manyong Moon and Sungsoo Song pay much attention to three historical actors working to advance Korea through science and technology: the government, corporations, and researchers. Moon traces the evolution of the first Korean government-funded research institute, the Korea Institute of Science and Technology (KIST), from its inception in 1966 to its development as a model for other government-funded research institutions created in the 1970s and 80s. Moon shows that the history of KIST is more than just another story of institutional growth. It encapsulates science and technology policies developed and implemented by the Korean government during the period of rapid industrialization. In this sense, KIST was and still is a successful exemplar of linking government officials, corporate leaders, and academic researchers. In contrast, Sungsoo Song takes us to see the changing corporate strategies in steel industry during a similar time span. The Pohang Iron and Steel Company (POSCO), established in 1968 as a public enterprise and completely privatized in 2000, exemplifies technology transfer as a historical process that involves overseas training (especially in Japan), efforts to become the first follower of advanced technologies, and strengthening of R&D function.

A closer look at the interactions among the historical actors reveals the intricate workings of power at different levels. Sulfikar Amir's study of the Indonesian case, for instance, illustrates the strength of the alliance between professional experts and government officials under the authoritarian regime that could maintain the stability of the technology-oriented national innovation system for some decades. The Korean government in the 1950s had much interest in boosting the capacity in science and technology but lacked the financial and political means to mobilize the nation's resources. It was only in the late 1960s that we can see the emergence of such a powerful alliance between technocrats and politicians under the military regime. Buhm Soon Park looks into Korea's early nuclear program that had a most pronounced technology gap from the outset. Who are nuclear experts? Who should decide the future direction of this program? What kind of bureaucracy should be formed for it? Analyzing the debates raised over the governance of the nuclear program, Park argues that the rhetoric of technonationalism served as an ideological weapon for the early technocrats, mostly the scientists-cum-administrators, to pursue their bureaucratic autonomy within the government. From 1968 on, Park shows, the military government co-opted this effort and laid out a clear bureaucratic arrangement by prescribing a division of labor between the research institute and the state-owned utility company (forerunner of the Korea Electric Power Company), the company that would play a leading role in the construction of commercial nuclear power plants.

Byung-Koo Kim's essay draws on his own experience as an engineer who made a seminal contribution to the development of Korea's standard nuclear reactor. Trained as a mechanical engineer at Caltech (Ph.D. 1972), Kim was scouted back to Korea as part of the reverse brain drain policy and spearheaded the task of developing nuclear fuel at Korea Atomic Energy Research Institute. He later became the project manager for designing the power reactor system, a technology central to a nuclear power plant. Before his retirement in 2008, he also worked as the director of the Technical Cooperation Department at IAEA. Kim's essay gives a vivid illustration of collective aspirations and individual ordeals involved in technology transfer—in a sense, the process of decontextualization and recontextualization of technology.

There is no doubt we need more case studies to fully grasp the meaning of the technology gap in Asia, i.e., how it functioned as a rhetorical tool to move people's minds, shape government policies, and change social relations. Collectively, I believe, the essays presented in this volume will serve as an invaluable starting point for further study.

Bridging the Technology Gap in Japan

Technology, Culture and Identity from the Late 19th to the 21st Century*

Morris Low

Introduction

This chapter examines Japanese attempts to bridge the technology gap with the West and more recently, its attempt to maintain the lead, in the face of fierce competition from Asian countries such as South Korea. The Japanese understood Western technology as something that they could graft onto "traditional" values. Japanese technological culture is seen as an amalgam of Western technology and Japanese culture which combines the strengths of both. This is reflected not only in the hybrid nature of Japanese technology today, but it is clearly evident in the late nineteenth century even when Japan was looking to the West for its know-how. This chapter examines why this was so. It asks to what extent

* In this chapter, Japanese names follow normal Japanese order of family name before given name. Where their names appear in Western order as authors of publications in English, that order is used.

Japanese technological culture and a tendency for hybridity was constructed and fostered. The concept of "technological culture" helps us to explore the relationship between technology and culture.[1]

The paper begins by focusing on the Imperial College of Engineering whose first principal was the Scotsman Henry Dyer(1848-1918). Fields that were taught there included: telegraphy and electrical engineering, architecture, and Western-style art. The Japanese ability to catch up and bridge the technology gap was evident at national industrial exhibitions which were held especially in Tokyo. But what is striking is how exhibitors drew on traditional agricultural and craft techniques to innovate, creating a Japanese technology that was often hybrid in nature. Over one hundred years later, "monozukuri" has become a buzz-word, part of a desire to recapture the creativity and prowess in making things that was so apparent in the Meiji period. But is this nostalgia for a Japan that was geared to catching up sufficient to propel Japan into the 21st century?

Wakon Yōsai

Japan's encounter with other industrial cultures was far more complicated than a mere transfer of science and technology. Japanese technological culture can be seen as an amalgam of Western technology and

1 See for example, J. Macgregor Wise, "Technological Culture," unpublished paper presented at the Asia Cultural Forum, (Gwangju, Korea, 2006).

Japanese culture which combines the strengths of both.[2] The idea of being able to separate Japanese culture from foreign influence can be traced back to the old idea of "*wakon kansai*" ("Japanese spirit, Chinese skills"). By 1854, however, when Sakuma Shōzan coined the phrase "*Tōyō no dōtoku, seiyō no geijutsu*" ("Eastern morality, Western techniques"), the Japanese were more interested in borrowing from the West. Sakuma tried to incorporate Western science and technology with a Confucian framework. It was through this hybridism that Japan would create a new order.[3] Both this slogan and the Meiji era (1868-1912) slogan "*wakon yōsai*" ("Japanese spirit, Western technology") are examples of how the Japanese dealt with the dilemma of the threat posed by modernity to cultural traditions. They are examples of how narratives about Japanese identity reflected (1) the need to catch up with the West and embrace a Western-inspired modernity, and (2) at the same time show concern regarding the effects of the introduction of foreign ideas and know-how. This concern continues to this very day. While such slogans do rely on outmoded dichotomies between Japan and "the West", they nevertheless articulate the idea that there is a "Japanese" technological culture that is somehow different from elsewhere that enables the Japanese to westernize (adopt Western technology) without becoming Western.

This hybridism can be seen in the hybrid nature of Japanese technology in the late nineteenth century when Japan was looking to the West for its know-how. Why was this so? To investigate this, I would

---

2 Morris Low, "Technological Culture" in *The Cambridge Companion to Modern Japanese Culture*, ed., Yoshio Sugimoto (Melbourne, 2009), 130-46.

3 John E. Van Sant, "Sakuma Shozan's Hegelian Vision for Japan," *Asian Philosophy*, 14 (2004): 277-92.

like to firstly focus on two Western-influenced institutions: the Imperial College of Engineering in Tokyo whose first principal was the Scotsman Henry Dyer (1848-1918)(appointed at the young age of 24),[4] and national industrial exhibitions which were held throughout Japan .

Imperial College of Engineering

The Imperial College of Engineering (1873-1886) was run by the Ministry of Public Works. Dyer was principal from 1873 through to 1882 when he returned to Scotland. A forerunner institution was the Kōgakuryō which had been established in 1871. It was known as this in Japanese until 1877 when it became known as the Kōbu Daigakkō. When the ministry was abolished in 1885, a few years after Dyer's return, control of the college was transferred to the Ministry of Education. In total, there were 211 graduates of the college who constituted an engineering elite. Their specializations were as follows: architecture (zōkagaku) (20), practical chemistry (25), metallurgy (5), civil engineering (45), mechanical engineering (39), mining (48), naval architecture (8), and telegraphy (21).[5] In 1886, it became the Faculty of Engineering at the Imperial University of Tokyo. In 1876, the Art School of the Imperial College of Engineering (Kōbu Bijutsu Gakkō) was established but was closed down in

4 Olive Checkland, "Henry Dyer at the Imperial College of Engineering in Tokyo, and Afterwards in Glasgow," in *Britain and Japan: Biographical Portraits*, Vol. III, ed., J.E. Hoare (Richmond, Surrey, 1999), 121-131.

5 Nobuhiro Miyoshi (trans. By Takuji and Aiko Sarada), *Henry Dyer: Pioneer of Engineering Education in Japan* (Folkestone, Kent, 2004), 136.

1883 against the backdrop of growing doubts about Japan's rapid westernization. This paper will briefly examine the departments of architecture and telegraphy, along with the school of art.

Gregory Clancey reminds us that the college was established to educate the sons of samurai, not artisans. Graduates of the college were required to work in the Ministry of Public Works or in government positions for at least seven years.[6] Although we can point to how some *daiku* (traditionally-trained carpenters) did hold important positions in the Ministry of Public Works,[7] there was nevertheless a class divide. A cartoon from Japan Punch (June 1874) shows Dyer in a horse-drawn carriage while despondent students are asked to do menial work such as cleaning their rooms, as punishment for misdemeanours.[8]

Telegraphy and the Beginnings of Electrical Engineering

Shortly after the Meiji Restoration in 1868, the British engineer George Miles Gilbert was hired to build a telegraph line between Tokyo and Yokohama, which he completed in January 1870 using mostly imported British equipment.[9] The Tokyo Telegraph School was established

6 Gregory Clancey, *Earthquake Nation: The Cultural Politics of Japanese Seismicity, 1868-1930* (Berkeley, 2006), 13, 20.

7 Ibid. 33.

8 Olive Checkland, *Britain's Encounter with Meiji Japan, 1868-1912* (Houndmills, Basingstoke, 1989), 77.

9 Simon Partner, *Assembled in Japan: Electrical Goods and the Making of the Japanese Consumer* (Berkeley, 1999), 11.

in 1871 and where Gilbert also taught. By May 1887, 1381 students had formally graduated from the school.[10]

In 1871, with the expansion of the network, it became necessary to establish a warehouse where equipment could also be repaired. The Austrian engineer Luis Schaefer provided some advice about how to produce communications equipment.[11] An apprentice in the Telegraph Bureau, Oki Kibatarō was one of Schaefer's students. In 1873, the Ministry of Public Works sought to overcome its dependence on foreign telegraph equipment by establishing a production division within the Telegraph Bureau. The elderly craftsman and entrepreneur Tanaka Hisashige, one of the founders of what would become Tōshiba, was commissioned by the Ministry to essentially copy the equipment. He set up a temporary workshop in Azabu, Tokyo where in 1873, he produced ten Henry telegraph devices and many Morse code telegraph machines.[12] In 1875, Tanaka established the Tanaka Engineering Works (Tanaka Seizōsho). He helped train other entrepreneurs such as Oki who went on to found what is now known as Oki Electric[13] and Miyoshi Shōichi (1853-1906)[14](who trained at the Tokyo Telegraph School). Others included Iwadare Kunihiko who had studied at the Imperial College of Engineering.[15] In 1898, Iwadare

10 Tsunekawa, Seiji, "Meiji Nihon ni okeru shoki denki gijutsusha no bunseki" ["An Analysis of the Early Electrical Engineers in Meiji Japan"], *Kagakushi kenkyū*, 42 (2003): 20-30, esp. 23.

11 Ibid., 23.

12 Oki Electric, *Progressive Spirit: The 120-Year History of Oki Electric* (Tokyo, 2002), 5.

13 Ibid.

14 Yuzo Takahashi, "The Evolution of Electrical Insulation Technology in Japan," *IEEE Electrical Insulation Magazine,* 10, no. 6 (Nov.-Dec. 1994): 10-16.

15 John M. Anderson, "Kunihiko Iwadare: Edison Apprentice and NEC Cofounder," *IEEE Power Engineering Review* (April 2001): 51.

founded the Nippon Electric Company (NEC) with Maeda Takeshiro who also trained at the Telegraph Technical School.[16]

William Ayrton (1847-1908) was the first professor of natural philosophy and telegraphy at the Imperial College of Engineering. From 1873 to 1878, he taught some twenty students who would each later write theses on telegraph-related topics. In addition, Ayrton taught several special students sent by the Telegraph Bureau of the Ministry of Public Works. Among them were students who had been trained at the Tokyo Telegraph School.[17] Thus, while some students had contact with Gilbert, Ayrton, and Tanaka, Ayrton was only able to formally train a very small number of advanced college graduates in telegraphy.

In contrast, the Tokyo Telegraph School and Tanaka were better able to meet the urgent need for telegraph engineers with their hands-on, practical approach to education. Although college graduates went on to fill important roles as educators, bureaucrats, and sometimes entrepreneurs, Tsunekawa Seiji has pointed out that the development of electrical technology has tended to rely more on craftsmen and artisans rather than college or university graduates.[18] This reflects differing opinions at the time of how best to train an engineer.

While Dyer sought to combine both a basic scientific education

16 Marie Anchordoguy, "Nippon Telegraph and Telephone Company (NTT) and the Building of a Telecommunications Industry in Japan," *Business History Review*, 75 (Autumn 2001): 507-541, esp. 510.

17 Yuzo Takahashi, "William Edward Ayrton at the Imperial College of Engineering in Tokyo: The First Professor of Electrical Engineering in the World," *IEEE Transactions on Education*, 33, no. 2 (May 1990): 198-205.

18 Tsunekawa, Seiji, "Meiji Nihon ni okeru shoki denki gijutsusha no bunseki" ["An Analysis of the Early Electrical Engineers in Meiji Japan"], *Kagakushi kenkyū*, 42 (2003): 20-30, esp. 30.

along with practical, on-the-job training, the college was not able to train engineers in sufficient numbers. As Janet Hunter has reported, there were only 131 graduate engineers working in private industry in Japan in 1890. As late as 1900, this figure had only increased to 385. Most of the engineers worked in heavy industry. In the important textile industry, there were only eighteen, formally-trained engineers. This figure rose to only seventy-seven in 1900.[19]

Architecture

Most architects were essentially apprentices who were trained in architects' offices and some studied at universities. The English architect Josiah Conder (1852-1920) who taught at the Imperial College of Engineering, was a product of both. In 1869, Conder entered the office of T. Roger Smith (1830-1903) who lectured at University College, London before becoming professor of architecture there. Conder attended lectures at University College and studied drawing at South Kensington Art School.[20] Conder and Smith were related. Smith's aunt was Conder's grandmother.[21]

Smith believed that British architects abroad needed to adapt Eu-

19 Janet Hunter, "British Training for Japanese Engineers: The Case of Kikuchi Kyōzō (1859-1942)," in *Britain and Japan, 1859-1991: Themes and Personalities,* eds., Sir Hugh Cortazzi and Gordon Daniels (London, 1991), 137-46.

20 Alice Y. Tseng, "Styling Japan: The Case of Josiah Conder and the Museum at Ueno, Tokyo," *Journal of the Society of Architectural Historians*, 63 (2004): 472-97.

21 Toshio Watanabe, "Japanese Imperial Architecture: From Thomas Roger Smith to Itō Chūta," in *Challenging Past and Present: The Metamorphosis of Nineteenth-Century Japanese Art*, ed., Ellen P. Conant (Honolulu, 2006), 238-53.

ropean styles to available materials and local contexts. It was through such adaptation that a new style would emerge. Exposure to the world via "foreign travel, photography, and the multiplication of all kinds of pictorial illustrations have made all the art of the past the property of the present."[22]

In 1874, after overseas travel, Conder entered the office of the gothic revivalist William Burges (1827-1881) who was an enthusiast of Japanese art and collected Japanese prints, ceramics, lacquerware and furniture.[23] Burges would no doubt have been delighted when Conder was appointed professor of architecture in Tokyo in 1876, at the same age that Dyer was: 24 years.[24] He arrived in Japan in 1877 and remained there until his death in 1920.

Given that a total of only twenty architects graduated from the Imperial College of Engineering, many buildings during the Meiji period were designed and constructed by men with expertise in timber buildings rather than formally trained architects who had studied brick-based Western-style architecture. This contributed to the rise of *giyōfū* (pseudo-Western-style) architecture which appeared Western but with indigenous elements.[25]

---

22 J. Mordaunt Crook, "Josiah Conder in England: Education, Training and Background," in *Josiah Conder: A Victorian Architect in Japan*, eds., Hiroyuki Suzuki, Terunobu Fujimori, and Tokuzu Hara (Tokyo, 1997), 26-28, esp. 26.

23 J. Mordaunt Crook, William Burges and the High Victorian Dream (London, 1981), 53; Dallas Finn, "Josiah Conder (1852-1920) and Meiji Architecture," in *Britain and Japan, 1859-1991: Themes and Personalities*, eds., Sir Hugh Cortazzi and Gordon Daniels (London, 1991), 86-93.

24 Crook, "Josiah Conder in England," 27.

25 Toshio Watanabe, "Josiah Conder's Rokumeikan: Architecture and National Representation in Meiji Japan," *Art Journal*, 55, no. 3 (Autumn 1996): 21-27.

Art and Industry

There was a strong belief in the 1870s that Western-style art could serve the nation and assist in the spread of knowledge. The Art School of the Ministry of Public Works (Kōbu Bijutsu Gakkō) was established in November 1876 as the first government school for Western-style art. It aimed to help Japanese industry adopt Western techniques and know-how. The school was part of the Imperial College of Engineering. Three Italian artists were employed as instructors in painting, sculpture, and architectural decoration. Although it was intended that the school foster the application of art in industry by helping to introduce Western techniques into traditional manufacturing, the focus shifted to education in the fine arts and it eventually closed in 1883.[26]

More successful in bring together art and industry was the German chemist Gottfried von Wagener (1831-1892). Wagener, like Conder, spent much of his career in Japan. Wagener worked there for twenty-four years. During this time, he introduced Japanese potters to Western glazes, firing techniques and production methods. In 1872, he was appointed a consultant by the Japanese government for the 1873 World Exposition in Vienna and assisted in preparing the art exhibits for that fair and the subsequent Philadelphia Centennial Exposition in 1876.[27] He later supervised the Kangōryō (Institute for the Encouragement of Industry

26 Yoshinori Amagai, "The Kobu Bijutsu Gakko and the Beginning of Design Education in Modern Japan," *Design Issues*, 19, no. 2 (Spring 2003): 35-44.

27 William Elliot Griffis, *The Mikado's Empire: A History of Japan from the Age of Gods to the Meiji Era (660 BC – AD 1872)* (originally published 1883; eight edition 1895)(Berkeley, 2006), 438.

and Commerce) and in the mid-1870s, encouraged the Ministry of Education to establish a Manufacturing School (Seisakugaku Kyōjo) at the Tokyo Kaisei Gakkō, a forerunner institution of the University of Tokyo. In 1878, he worked at the Seimikyoku chemical research institute in Kyoto, helping to improve the traditional arts of cloisonné, glass, textile-dyeing and ceramics. Not only did he encourage the Japanese to value their traditional arts, but he suggested that they use these skills to introduce technologies from overseas.[28] A good example of this is how Fukagawa Eizaemon VIII succeeded in manufacturing the first Japanese porcelain insulator for telegraphic communication in 1870. He later established the Kōransha company at Arita in Kyushu in 1875.[29]

Wagener had a number of teaching positions at various institutions over the years, and made a major contribution to technical education in Japan by improving traditional arts and industries, quite independent of Dyer and the largely British-staffed Imperial College of Engineering.[30]

Both Conder and Wagener sought to innovate, but drew on the past for inspiration. While we might see the "practical, pragmatic eclecticism"[31] that Josiah Conder learnt from T. Roger Smith as being commonsense, we need to remember how his Japanese clients often wanted architecture that appeared Western. Similarly, we shouldn't for-

28 Nobuhiro Miyoshi (trans. By Takuji and Aiko Sarada), *Henry Dyer: Pioneer of Engineering Education in Japan* (Folkestone, Kent, 2004), 149.

29 Yuzo Takahashi, "The Evolution of Electrical Insulation Technology in Japan," *IEEE Electrical Insulation Magazine*, 10, no. 6 (Nov.-Dec. 1994): 10-16, esp. 10; Koransha Co. Ltd., "Company History", online at http://www.koransha.co.jp/english/. Viewed 12 January 2010.

30 Clare Pollard, *Master Potter of Meiji Japan: Makuzu Kōzan (1842-1916) and His Workshop* (Oxford, 2002).

31 Crook, "Josiah Conder in England," 26.

get that in the early Meiji period, craftsmen had lost their patrons and their work was often denigrated in favour of Western products. Wagener championed their work by establishing modern workshops where their products could be produced in larger quantities, using designs that appealed to the taste of foreigners. Wagener showcased their work at Vienna, helping to create international interest in traditional arts and crafts. [32]

Role of Expositions

In 1876, the "porcelain manufactory" Kōransha won a certificate of merit at the Philadelphia Centennial Exposition. Included in the company's display were flower vases of various sizes by Y. Fukagawa. What is likely to have attracted the attention of the judges was Fukagawa's 10 foot-high vase! The tea and coffeee services and lamp vases which were exhibited clearly show how the Fukagawa family were targetting Western taste and the foreign export market.[33] Kōransha exhibited a low-pressure, porcelain insulator at the 1877 National Industrial Exhibition in Tokyo where it received a certificate of merit, and the company won the Gold Prize at the Paris Exposition Universelle in 1878.[34] The company would

32 Gunhild Avitabile, "Gottfried Wagener (1831-1892)," in *Meiji no takara: Ronbun hen [Treasures of Imperial Japan. Selected Essays]*, ed., O.R. Impey (London, 1995), 98-122; Monika Bincsik, "European Collectors and Japanese Merchants of Lacquer in Old Japan," *Journal of the History of Collections* (2008): 1-20.

33 Japanese Commission, *International Exhibition, 1876: Official Catalogue of the Japanese Section, and Descriptive Notes on the Industry and Agriculture of Japan* (Philadelphia, 1876), 15.

34 Koransha Co. Ltd., "Company History", online at http://www.koransha.co.jp/english/. Viewed 12 January 2010.

go on to compete and win prizes at other international expositions which provided useful opportunities for promoting and selling Kōransha products.

We can also point to the success of other Japanese artisans. At the First National Industrial Exhibition, the award for the best invention, the Hōmon Hōshō (Firebird Prize) went to Gaun Tatchi (1842-1900) from the Shinshū region, for a "rattling spindle" ("*garabō*") device for spinning yarn.[35] Cotton was packed into bamboo or metal tubes, drawn out from receptacles, and twisted onto rollers to become yarn.[36] Visitors certainly learnt by seeing. The device was easy to copy and as there was no patent law at the time, little profit flowed to Gaun.[37] Gaun's machine could be reproduced without too much difficulty by carpenters.[38] Gaun exhibited at the Second and Third National Industrial Exhibitions, held respectively in 1881 and 1890. He won prizes at all three.[39] However, due to competition from Western spinning machines, the popularity of the

---

35 Also sometimes referred to as Gaun Tatsuchi, Gaun Tokimune or Gaun Tatsumune. For further information, see Ishida, Shōji, "Dai Ikkai Naikoku Kangyō Hakurankai shuppin: Gaun Tatchi no menbōki fukugenki no sekkei" ["An Exhibit at the First National Industrial Exhibition: The Design of a Reconstruction of a Gaun Tatchi Cotton Spinning Machine"], *Anjō-shi Rekishi Hakubutsukan kenkyū kiyō [Research Bulletin of the Anjō City Historical Museum]*, no. 2 (1995), online version.

36 For an illustration of the machine see Tessa Morris-Suzuki, *The Technological Transformation of Japan: From the Seventeenth to the Twenty-First Century* (Cambridge, 1994), 90.

37 Sara Harris, "The Making of an IP Nation" Japan Inc (Dec. 2002), online version. http://www.japaninc.com/article.php?articleID=951/. Viewed 27 May 2013.

38 Morris-Suzuki, 83, 90.

39 For details, see Kitano, Susumu, *Gaun Tokimune to garabōki: Hatsumei no bunka isan; wa bōshi, wa nuno no nazo o saguru (Gaun Tokimune and the Garabōki Spinning Machine: The Cultural Heritage of Inventions, Solving the Puzzle of Japanese Spun Cotton and Japanese Cloth)*(Tokyo, 1994); Miyashita, Kazuo, *Gaun Tatchi: Garabōki 100 nen no ashiato o tazunete (Gaun Tatchi: Tracing 100 Years of the Garabōki Spinning Machine)*(Matsumoto, 1993).

Gaun machine declined after 1890.

Tessa Morris-Suzuki has pointed out how most of the exhibits at the first exhibition drew on traditional agricultural and craft techniques. The Tokyo Telegraph School-trained Miyoshi Shōichi displayed a treadle-type multi-cocoon reeling machine which he invented by for the Tomioka Filature Plant in Gunma prefecture. It won a certificate of merit. Though there were "modern" attractions, such as a steam locomotive, even in the machinery division exhibits tended to be made of wood and powered by waterwheels.

The exhibitions displayed the old along with the new, in the hope of promoting new products that might draw on traditional technologies. This extended even to the fine arts. In this way, modernization in Japan was not simply a process of westernization. Nor was it simply a rejection of the past. The Ministry of Education in particular saw historical artifacts as "cultural assets that should be protected for the future."[40] Exhibitions juxtaposed things Western with indigenous artifacts and technologies.

> The exposition shows that the Japanese have changed, modified, revised, and, in many cases, have improved upon American and European productions. Some Japanese manufacturers have received a jaunty touch of Americanism, and some European and American productions have been enlivened with a genius Japanese. Sometimes the experimental combination is a success. Often it is a failure.[41]

40 Kazuto Sawada, "Second National Industrial Exhibition," National Museum of Japanese History, Sakura City, Chiba, Japan. Online at http://www.rekihaku.ac.jp/e-rekihaku/130/cover.html

41 R.R., "Japan's Big Exposition," *Chicago Daily Tribune*, 28 June 1890, 9.

It is not surprising that interaction occurred, with modification and adaptation occurring to meet Japanese needs and conditions.[42] This reflected how the Japanese saw their cultural identity, a hybrid sense of self which appeared outwardly Western. We can see this in Oki Kibatarō's Microsound device which was exhibited at the Second National Industrial Exhibition in 1881. The device was an Edison-type telephone which used carbon powder instead of carbon rods. It won a second-place award for innovation.[43] The success of Tanaka, Oki and Miyoshi show how many engineers who worked in the production division of the Telegraph Bureau later left to work in the private sector where they established companies that specialized in the manufacture of electrical equipment and machinery.[44]

Towards a Japanese Technology

In 1886, Conder delivered an address before the Association of Japanese Architects where he defended the idea of the Imperial College of Engineering having had an art school that employed Italian teachers. He argued that

> I see very little fear of Japan losing national type and character in the

42 Janet Hunter, "Institutional Revolution: The Case of Meiji Japan," in *Institutional Change in Japan*, eds., Magnus Blomstrom and Sumner La Croix (London, 2006), part 1, chapter 2.

43 Oki Printing Solutions, "Our Innovations: 1880s," online at http://www.okiprinting-solutions.com/1880.html

44 Oki Electric, *Progressive Spirit: The 120-Year History of Oki Electric* (Tokyo, 2002), 5.

> art which she will eventually develop provided that the natural artistic instincts of the people are kept alive. But if, out of terror of the bugbear called "hybridity", those responsible for the national education hesitate to establish proper instruction in the arts – if they favour only a narrow and seclusive curriculum of art education, it is to be feared that the country may eventually lose her aesthetic capabilities.[45]

In 1933, the novelist Tanizaki Junichirō wrote an essay entitled "In Praise of Shadows". It begins with his reflections on:

> What incredible pains the fancier of traditional architecture must take when he sets out to build a house in pure Japanese style, striving somehow to make electric wires, gas pipes, and water lines harmonize with the austerity of Japanese rooms.[46]

He goes on to speculate about what might have been:

> But had we devised independently at least the more practical sorts of inventions, this could not but have had profound influence upon the conduct of our everyday lives, and even upon government, religion, art, and business. The Orient quite conceivably could have opened up a

45 Josiah Conder, an address delivered before the Association of Japanese Architects on 14 July 1886, *The Japan Weekly Mail*, 28 August 1886, 213-216, esp. 214. Cited in Toshio Watanabe, "Japanese Imperial Architecture: From Thomas Roger Smith to Itō Chūta," in *Challenging Past and Present: The Metamorphosis of Nineteenth-Century Japanese Art*, ed. Ellen P. Conant (Honolulu: University of Hawaii Press, 2006), 238-253, esp. 246.

46 Junichirō Tanizaki, (trans. by Thomas J. Harper and Edward G. Seidensticker), *In Praise of Shadows* (London, 2001), 5.

world of technology entirely its own.[47]

While a truly "Japanese technology" that Tanizaki mused about was not practical in late nineteenth-century Japan, we have seen how hybrid products were very much part of technological culture. This was partly a result of a desire to make the most of existing resources in the form of traditional arts and industries, as well as personnel, given the lack of formally-trained engineers and architects.

From 1874, well-to-do Japanese built Western-style reception rooms which were appended to homes that were otherwise built in the style of Edo-period samurai residences. Such separation of the home into more formal areas to entertain guests or do business, and more private family areas, continue to this day. They reflect what has been called a "two-layer lifestyle" (*nijū seikatsu*)[48] that reflects the hybrid nature of everyday life and technological culture in Japan today.

Since the nineteenth century, the abovementioned slogan "*wakon yōsai*" ("Japanese spirit, Western technology") allowed the Japanese to create a space for their own culture and to develop a sense of identity based on the relationship between Western technology and Japanese cultural traditions. The relationship between the two have fluctuated at times, especially during the Meiji period. In the late 1870s, the emphasis on Western technology gave way to a type of cultural nationalism.

47 Tanizaki, 14.

48 Don Hoon Choi, "Domesticated Modern: Hybrid Houses in Meiji Japan, 1870-1900," PhD dissertation, University of California, Berkeley, 2003, 17.

Post-World War II Japan

In the wake of defeat in World War II, *wakon* became discredited and was largely replaced from the late 1950s by rampant consumerism. With rising confidence in Japanese technology, people sought to account for Japanese success and interest in *wakon* could be seen in advertising and accounts of the Japanese economic "miracle" from the 1960s.

Japanese technological culture is thus seen as an amalgam of Western technology and Japanese culture which combines the strengths of both. The waxing and waning of *wakon* to provide a window to the Japanese embrace of modernity, and the concomitant confidence of the Japanese people in themselves and at times their traditions. Some writers point to the importance of wakon and Japanese aesthetics in the success of Japanese products not only in the Meiji period but also the post-World War II period.

Scholars have differed in terms of their view of the relationship of technology to the larger culture in which it is immersed. This has often been characterized in terms of not only how Japanese culture has contributed to technological change and innovation but also extends to examining how aspects of Japanese society and culture have been deficient or held back Japan's embrace of technology.[49]

In *Why Has Japan Succeeded: Western Technology and the Japanese Ethos* (1982), the economist Michio Morishima asks the question of how it was that the Japanese, who possess a "remarkably idiosyncratic ethos",

49 Ian Inkster, "Introduction: Culture and Technology in Japan," in *Culture and Technology in Modern Japan*, eds., Ian Inkster and Fumihiko Satofuka (London, 2000), 1-21.

were able to "gain such control over the industrial techniques produced by the West".[50] He points to the importance of Confucianism in Japan and how it differed from Confucianism in China. The latter was humanistic whereas the former was nationalistic. Combined with Shintoism, it provided a powerful doctrine that helped propel Japan on a path of development that was very different from China's at the time.

Much has been written over the years about the role of government policies in Japan's rapid economic growth. The literature has been dominated by classics such as Chalmers Johnson's *MITI and the Japanese Miracle* (1982),[51] Daniel I. Okimoto's Between *MITI and the Market* (1989)[52] and Scott Callon's Divided Sun (1995).[53] Takatoshi Ito (1992),[54] in his well-known text on *The Japanese Economy*, draws attention to how the Japanese were able to successfully adopt and adapt elements of other cultures.

This type of argument is extended into the post-World War II period to describe Japan's "economic miracle". It enables the Japanese to praise American technological superiority and at the same time carve out a sense of their own identity based on a propensity to assimilate others. Japan can be said to have shown a strong technological orientation, epitomized by the spectacular growth of the car and electronic industries

---

50 Michio Morishima, *Why Has Japan Succeeded: Western Technology and the Japanese Ethos* (Cambridge, 1982), viii.

51 Chalmers Johnson, *MITI and the Japanese Miracle* (Stanford, 1982).

52 Daniel I. Okimoto, *Between MITI and the Market: Japanese Industrial Policy for High Technology* (Stanford, 1989).

53 Scott Callon, *Divided Sun: MITI and the Breakdown of Japanese High-Tech Industrial Policy, 1975-1993* (Stanford, 1995).

54 Takatoshi Ito, *The Japanese Economy* (Cambridge, Mass., 1992).

in the post-World War II years. It is possible to argue that a tendency towards a technological culture in Japan has meant that not only have the Japanese quickly embraced new technologies but they have been more open to borrowing from other cultures in general.

Partner (1999)[55] argues that the USA was pivotal to the development of the electrical goods industry in Japan. He points to the importance of the Allied Occupation of Japan (1945-52); the role of American-style anti-communism in promoting television in Japan; the role-model that the USA provided as a consumer society; the transfer of American technology after the war; and the emergence of the USA as a market for electrical components.

In the 1960s, advertisements increasingly suggested that the Japanese should take pride in the products that were made in Japan by manufacturers such as Sony, Sanyo and Matsushita. Such technology was related to Japanese aesthetics, history of craftsmanship and closeness to nature. Whereas the products were originally heralded as symbols of Americanization not long after the end of the Allied Occupation of Japan (1945-52), increased Japanese confidence in themselves (at least at home) changed the discourse to one which emphasized Japanese culture.[56]

This discourse has continued to the present day. In 1990, Sheridan Tatsuno argued that the Japanese are more "adaptive, holistic, and

55 Simon Partner, *Assembled in Japan: Electrical Goods and the Making of the Japanese Consumer* (Berkeley, 1999).

56 Yoshimi, Shunya, "Television and Nationalism: Historical Change in the National Domestic TV Formation of Postwar Japan," *European Journal of Cultural Studies*, 6 (2003): 459-87, esp. 474.

cyclical" than Westerners.[57] The Japanese, he felt, need to make more technological breakthroughs of their own (rather than borrow from the U.S.) and draw on their cultural heritage, especially aesthetic tendencies such as miniaturization. The Japanese, it is said, like combining ideas to make hybrid technologies, fusing old ideas with new, to make new products.

Such beliefs have fuelled the idea of a *monozukuri* tradition in Japan. Rather than the logical, scientific mode of thinking which is common in the West, it has been argued that the Japanese are characterized by a more holistic approach which encourages them to use their experience and professional intuition to solve problems, rather than rely on scientific reasoning and understanding. This, it is argued, can be seen in the work of skilled craftsmen in Japan.[58]

With the bursting of the bubble in 1990, Japanese leaders recognized that there was a growing technology gap in software and Internet-related fields. With the the shift of Japanese manufacturing to other parts of Asia in the 1990s, more and more of "Japanese" technology was being produced overseas. By 1996, it was estimated that over a third of Japanese car stereos and VCRs, more than two-thirds of colour televisions, and a large eighty per cent of hi-fi audio equipment made by Japanese companies were produced elsewhere. China and other Asian countries effectively provide the world with Japanese electrical appliances.[59]

---

57 Sheridan M. Tatsuno, *Created in Japan: From Imitators to World-Class Innovators* (New York, 1990), 15-16.

58 Kozo Saito, Abraham J. Salazar, Kenneth G. Kreafle and Eric A. Grulke, "Hitozukuri and Monozukuri: Centuries' Old Eastern Philosophy to Seek Harmony with Nature," *Interdisciplinary Information Sciences*, 17, no. 1 (2011): 1-9, esp. 8.

59 Russell Skelton, "Japan Goes to Asia, Where It's Cheaper," *The Sydney Morning Herald*, 27 July 1996, 34.

Maintaining the Lead

In response to the shift of Japanese manufacturing offshore in the 1990s, the term "*monozukuri*" came to be used in Japan to draw attention to the need to value the art of manufacturing and to nurture the creativity involved in making things. There has been a desire to rekindle the national pride associated with the export of Japanese consumer technologies in the postwar period and a perception that the Japanese need to recapture the values associated with traditional arts and crafts of the Edo and Meiji periods. It is only by valuing the Japanese approach to manufacturing things that the Japanese feel that they can meet the challenge posed by the rise of South Korea and more recently China.

It is no coincidence that the use of the term "*monozukuri*" increased in the second half of the 1990s, when the Japanese economy shrank and many lamented the lost decade of the 1990s.[60] By the mid-1990s, it was agreed by many that Japan had to re-orient itself away from being a "catch-up" system which tended not to emphasize creativity, risk-taking, and entrepreneurialism . Being a manufacturing nation was not good enough. Japan had to transform itself into an inventor nation if it was to secure its future.[61]

In the late 1990s, there was concern expressed by those in government, industry and academia, that something needed to be done. Book

60 Risaburo Nezu, "Industrial Policy in Japan", *Journal of Industry, Competition and Trade*, 7 (2007): 229-43, 229-30.

61 Marie Anchordoguy, "Japan at a Technological Crossroads: Does Change Support Convergence Theory?," *Journal of Japanese Studies*, 23, no. 2 (Summer 1997): 363-97.

titles such as "*Monozukuri*" *kakumei (Monozukuri Revolution)*(1998)[62] and *Saraba "seizōgyō": Nihon no monozukuri wa kō kawaru!* (*Goodbye "Manufacturing": Japanese Monozukuri Will Change in This Way!*) (1999) reflect the widespread interest in the issue.[63] Such was the concern that a *Monozukuri Kondankai* (Monozukuri Colloquium) was convened. The colloquium, held at the official residence of the Prime Minister of Japan, met five times from late 1999 through to the first half of 2000.[64]

Prime Minister Obuchi Keizō convened the colloquium which was attended by three cabinet deputy secretaries, and chaired by Professor Karatsu Hajime (Tōkai University). The other ten distinguished academics and businessmen who attended the meetings were Akikusa Naoyuki (President, Fujitsū), Umehara Takeshi (Adviser, International Research Center for Japanese Studies), Okuda Hiroshi (Chairman, Toyota Motor Corporation), Kagono Tadao (Kobe University), Seki Mitsuhiro (Hitotsubashi University), Nishizawa Jun'ichi (Iwate Prefectural University), Maeda Matabei (President, Japanese Society for Quality Control), Makino Noboru (Adviser, Mitsubishi Research Institute), Yamada Shinjirō (President, Incs Inc.), and Richard C. Koo (Chief Economist, Nomura Research Institute). The five meetings culminated

62 Fuji Sōgō Kenkyūjo Sangyō Chōsabu, *"Monozukuri" kakumei [Monozukuri Revolution]* (Tokyo, 1998).

63 Nihon Keizai Shinbun ed., *Saraba "seizōgyō": Nihon no monozukuri wa kō kawaru! [Goodbye "Manufacturing": Japanese Monozukuri Will Change in This Way!]* (Tokyo, 1999).

64 See Monozukuri Kondankai, "Dai ikkai monozukuri kondankai giji gaiyō," ["Summary of the Proceedings of the Monozukuri Colloquium Meeting No. 1"], 24 December 1999; Monozukuri Kondankai, "Dai nikai monozukuri kondankai giji yōshi" ["Summary of the Proceedings of the Monozukuri Colloquium Meeting No. 2"], 24 January 2000; Monozukuri Kondankai, "Dai sankai monozukuri kondankai giji yōshi" ["Summary of the Proceedings of the Monozukuri Colloquium Meeting No. 3"], 24 February 2000; Monozukuri Kondankai, "Dai yonkai monozukuri kondankai giji yōshi" ["Summary of the Proceedings of the Monozukuri Colloquium Meeting No. 4"], 23 March 2000. All held at the Official Residence of the Prime Minister of Japan, Tokyo.

in the production of a proposal[65] which was tabled at the last meeting on 16 May 2000, held just two days after Obuchi's death. Although still held at the official residence, it was presided over by the new prime minister, Mori Yoshiro.[66]

The *monozukuri* fervour in Japan which has been emphasizing the need for craftsmanship has been criticized by some as being more myth than substance and contributing to a nationalistic discourse akin to the Nihonjinron literature about the so-called uniqueness of the Japanese.[67] The Japanese Government has regularly been using the buzzword of *monozukuri* in its White Papers on manufacturing,[68] not least because in some fields such as electronics, the Japanese appear to have fallen behind their Asian competitors.

What will it take for Japan to transform itself into a real world leader? The continuing bias towards hardware and *monozukuri* has been at the cost of innovation in software and content. Indeed, the interest in *monozukuri* is seen as a nostalgic yearning for a bygone, analogue era. Increasingly, it is said that the real cutting edge is in the digital world which emphasizes networks. Dujarric and Hagiu argue that most digital

---

65 Monozukuri Kondankai, "Monozukuri kondankai teigen" ["Proposal of the Monozukuri Colloquium"], 16 May 2000.

66 Monozukuri Kondankai, "Dai gokai monozukuri kondankai giji yōshi" ["Summary of the Proceedings of the Monozukuri Colloquium Meeting No. 5"], 16 May 2000, Official Residence of the Prime Minister of Japan, Tokyo.

67 Mon-Han Tsai, "The Myth of Monozukuri: Manufactured Manufacturing Ideology", ITEC Working Paper Series, no. 06-04 (March 2006), Institute for Technology, Enterprise and Competitiveness, Doshisha University, Kyoto.

68 Japanese Government, Ministry of Economy, Trade and Industry, Ministry of Health, Labour and Welfare, Ministry of Education, Culture, Sports, Science and Technology, Summary of the White Paper on Manufacturing Industries (Monodzukuri) 2010. Online at: http://www.meti.go.jp/english/report/data/Monodzukuri2010_01.pdf

devices are in large part services rather than pure products of the past.[69]

The Japanese lack software packages for personal computers that can compete with Microsoft Windows, but Japanese companies are strong in computer games and other specific applications.[70] We only need to look at Nintendo and Sony to find examples. Robert Dujarric and Andrei Hagiu concede that the Japanese are unlikely to be able to replicate Silicon Valley, but there is real technological innovation in mobile telephony and anime that the Japanese should capitalize on.[71] Digital products that have emerged out of Silicon Valley have been described by Fujimoto Takahiro as "open-modular products" and it was these products that grew in importance in the 1990s.[72]

In contrast, the Japanese have excelled at products based on closed-integral architecture such as automobiles, motorcycles, consumer electronics, cameras, and games software. I recently walked into my local Sony Centre in Brisbane, Australia, where I live, in the hunt for a new notebook or laptop computer. I had toyed with the idea of buying an Apple iPad but found that it didn't meet my needs with respect to word processing.

Sony's brand power got me in the door but I was surprised to find that most of the computers branded Sony were not made in Japan, apart from the top-of-the-line models. The local sales team at the store were knowledgable but the products they had to sell were not cost competitive.

---

69 Robert Dujarrac and Andrei Hagiu, "Capitalizing on Innovation: The Case of Japan", *Harvard Business School Working Paper*, no. 09-114 (2009).

70 Fujimoto, Takahiro, "A Twenty-First Century Strategy for Japanese Manufacturing", *Japan Echo*, 31, no. 1 (Feburary, 2004): 20-25.

71 Dujarrac and Hagiu.

72 Fujimoto.

I bought a cheap Hewlett Packard Mini Notebook computer elsewhere instead and later augmented it with the purchase of an Apple iPad tablet computer.

In recent years, the electronics industry in Japan has declined as other companies have produced more innovative products, sometimes manufacturing cheaper versions of products that had originally been developed in Japan.[73] It is not surprising that Samsung surpassed Sony in the BusinessWeek/Interbrand top global brand rankings for the first time back in 2005.[74] Apple's iPad has been popular in Japan, but its touch-screen display and processor are made by Samsung Electronics Co.[75]

In 2010, the rising yen prompted Renault-Nissan to increase auto production in South Korea and reduce its reliance on manufacturing in Japan.[76] Increasing competition from lower-cost countries such as South Korea and China is making it very difficult for Japanese companies to compete. The recent recall of cars by Toyota, considered one of the greatest practitioners of monozukuri, suggests that all is not well in Japanese manufacturing and that there are opportunities for Japan's rivals to take the lead in some key industries.

In today's globalized world, it is impossible to confine skilled workers to national borders. The downsizing of Japan's electronics industry has

---

73 Daiskuke Wakabayashi, "iPad a "Game-Changer" in Tokyo's Electronics Industry," *The Australian*, 1 June 2010, 38.

74 Interbrand, "BusinessWeek/Interbrand Annual Ranking of the 100 Top Global Brands: Samsung Surpasses Sony for the First Time, Taking over the No. 20 Spot," press release, 21 July 2005.

75 Arik Hesseldahl, "Teardown of Apple's Tablet Reveals the Sum of Its Parts," *The Sydney Morning Herald*, 13 April 2010, 10.

76 Vivian Salama, "Yen Drives Renault to Korea," *Australian Financial Review*, 1 September 2010, 17.

been accompanied by the loss of thousands of Japanese engineers to Taiwan, South Korea, China, and Singapore where Japanese technological expertise, especially in semiconductors, is highly prized.[77] These Japanese engineers have certainly helped China to lift its technological prowess and previously such assistance was considered a type of aid. What some see as a "brain drain" often consists of engineers who have difficulty finding jobs in Japan once they reach close to retirement age. Indeed, these engineers see themselves as contributing to the improvement of Sino-Japan relations.[78] However you may view it, their work is certainly contributing to a greater awareness among Japanese that their futures are tied to Asia. But the outflow of know-how is raising concerns about whether Japan will be able to maintain its lead in areas like electronics.

To combat "technology leakage", the Japanese Government has advised that Japanese companies should keep their production bases in Japan where possible, especially if the operations relate to core technology. When it is necessary to shift manufacturing off-shore, it is advised that overseas base should be majority-owned by Japanese. Technology leakage, we are told, occurs not only through products but by people, either currently employed or retired. Is Japan fighting a losing battle in trying to stem the flow of technological know-how? The same report informs us that even in the case of Japan's traditional craft industry (which is at the heart of *monozukuri* and which so impressed Westerners in the Meiji period), cheap imports are making inroads and local production has plunged to one-

---

77 Martin Fackler, "A Japanese Export: Talent; Technologists See Brighter Prospects in Other Parts of Asia," *The New York Times*, 24 May 2007, C1, C5.

78 Yasuyuki Nishii, Koichi Furuya and Jun Wakamatsu, "Engineers in China Defend Their Actions, " *The Asahi Shimbun* (English edition), no. 18190 (7 Dec. 2010), 1.

third of its peak.[79]

Today, the technological sophistication that we had previously associated with the Japanese has become more widespread elsewhere, and firms in many countries attempt to exploit opportunities as they arise. Rather than use the words "Made in Japan", it might be more appropriate to label many products as having been "Designed in Japan" or even "Inspired by Japan". *Wakon yōsai* has provided a useful way of understanding how the Japanese have defined themselves with respect to technology and to the West. When they are confident about themselves, they point to the importance of cultural traditions and when they are more despondent, they point to inadequacies and how Japanese culture is deficient. But the world is an increasingly complicated place and our sense of identity is more fluid.

Japan, having bridged the technology gap, can no longer simply borrow technologies from elsewhere. In the past, slogans such as *wakon yōsai* were sufficient when Japan was seeking to catch up with the West and maintain a sense of its own identity — an example of the "discursive construction of Japaneseness as the skillful domestication of foreign influence".[80] But now Japan needs to develop its own technologies. Buzzwords such as *monozukuri* are useful as a practical, defence strategy (much like *wakon yōsai* was during the Meiji period) to maintain Japanese confidence in their prowess in manufacturing at a time when it is threatened,

79 Japanese Government, Ministry of Economy, Trade and Industry, Ministry of Health, Labour and Welfare, Ministry of Education, Culture, Sports, Science and Technology, Summary of the White Paper on Manufacturing Industries (Monodzukuri) 2010. Online at: http://www.meti.go.jp/english/report/data/Monodzukuri2010_01.pdf

80 Koichi Iwabuchi, *Recentering Globalization: Popular Culture and Japanese Transnationalism* (Durham, N.C., 2002), 219.

but whether it is sufficient to instill creativity, a strong work ethic, self-discipline and nurture an entrepreneurial spirit among young Japanese is doubtful. But it is a dilemma that South Korea, and in time China, will also increasingly have to face: how to lead once you have caught up.

The dilemma today is how Japanese firms can regain their competitive advantage and move away from attempting to emulate other Japanese firms that are manufacturing a proliferation of similar products with too many features for too many market segments. This was a legacy of the postwar period when intense domestic competition was encouraged as a springboard for later export success.[81] Today, however, the emphasis on *monozukuri* can lead to a naive belief in the importance of maintaining domestic employment in manufacturing at all costs.[82] Overemphasis of its importance masks the real shift of Japanese industry to the service sectors.

Monozukuri emphasises the building of long-term relationships and the accumulation of skills and know-how within companies and their partners. While this concept has, in the past, been interpreted in terms of the need to upgrade domestic manufacturing capability, it might more usefully be expanded to include building a capability overseas through the spread of Japanese business models.[83] Indeed, this appears to be the way that Japanese companies are managing to remain competitive. Thirty

---

81 Risaburo Nezu, "Industrial Policy in Japan, " *Journal of Industry, Competition and Trade*, 7 (2007): 229-43, esp. 239.

82 Hiroshi Shimizu, "Inove-shon no Sōshutsu," book review, *Social Science Japan Journal* (20 December 2010), advance access online, viewed 30 April 2011.

83 Kenichi Ohno, "Avoiding the Middle-Income Trap: Renovating Industrial Policy Formulation in Vietnam," *ASEAN Economic Bulletin*, vol. 26, No. 1 (2009): 25-43, esp. 30-31.

per cent of their manufacturing now is done overseas. For Toyota, often cited as the epitome of *monozukuri*, the figure for its vehicles is almost double: a high 58%. Overseas production results in higher profit margins and greater access to increasingly wealth Asian consumers. Whereas previously, it could be argued that Japanese firms retained much of their know-how and judiciously maintained a technology gap between their factories in Japan and those abroad, it has been reported that three quarters of Japanese-owned overseas plants enjoy the same technical level as those in Japan.[84]

The discussion of "technology gap" in this chapter has tended to focus on Japan's attempts to catch up with the West, and its efforts to compete with other Asian nations such as South Korea and China. We also need to acknowledge that there are technology gaps within Japan, especially between Tokyo and its rival city Osaka, as well as the rest of Japan. Although the three regions around the cities of Tokyo, Osaka and Nagoya dominate manufaturing, Tokyo leads in many sectors. Tokyo is an education hub and there is a concentration of R&D and cultural facilities as well as administrative functions in the capital. It is a major communications node and most foreign-affiliated corporations establish their headquarters in Tokyo, rather than Osaka. Despite some attempts at decentralization such as the relocation of national R&D laboratories to Tsukuba Science City, industry has not followed.[85] What's more, the

84 "Japanese Manufacturers Leaving Home, " *The Economist* 397, no. 8709 (20 Nov. 2010): 71-72.

85 Hajime Eto, "Obstacles to Emergence of High/New Technology Parks, Ventures and Clusters in Japan," *Technological Forecasting and Social Change*, 72 (2005): 359-73, esp. 362.

aging of Japan's population is exacerbating the differences between the capital which attracts job-seeking young people and the rest of the country.[86]

Some see the primacy of Tokyo as having been a legacy of Japan's developmental state. In the postwar period, the Tokyo-based bureaucracy sought to influence the private sector through administrative guidance and incentives. The concentration of government ministries and finance in the nation's capital has meant that corporations such as Sharp, Matsushita and Sanyo which are still based in Osaka see the centrality of Tokyo as a problem.[87]

Conclusion

Calls for the revitalization of the Japanese economy through the promotion of *monozukuri* are a nostalgic attempt to strengthen Japan's manufacturing capability.[88] If we look at Japan's industralization in the late nineteenth century, we can certainly see Japanese ingenuity and creativity at work. Then as now, hybridity was a feature of Japanese technological culture. Japan has now caught up with the West, so it is not only a case of *wakon yōsai*, but a question of maintaining its leadership within the context of increased technological capabilities in South Korea and

86 Nezu, "Industrial Policy in Japan, " 237.

87 Richard Child Hill and Kuniko Fujita, "Osaka's Tokyo Problem," *International Journal of Urban and Regional Research*, 19 (1995): 181-93.

88 See for example Kazuo Sato, "Monozukuri wa hitozukuri/Monozukuri Bushidō" ["Monozukuri is Human Resource Development/Monozukuri Bushidō"], *Journal of the Japanese Society for Engineering Education*, 54, no. 5 (2006): 11-14.

China. The technology gaps that Japan now faces in the 21st century are of a different sort compared to the 19th and 20th centuries: competing with Asian neighbours and dealing with the gap between Tokyo and the rest of the nation.

Accelerated Transformation

High Technology, Nationalism, and Developmental Authoritarianism in Indonesia, 1966-1998

Sulfikar Amir

Introduction

In early 1970s, Indonesia startled the world with its entry into high technology competition through establishing its very own aircraft manufacturer. Like other newly industrialized Asian countries, Indonesia followed suit by harnessing oil revenues. However, the New Order regime's developmental trajectory was unique. It emphasized particularly the role of high-tech production as a means to accelerate industrialization. As such, the New Order placed massive efforts in developing high technologies as a means to accelerate tranformations of both the economy and society. The ultimate goal is to elevate Indonesia's position in the global economy to be of equal standing with other developed nations. Thus, financial, intellectual, and political resources were tremendously channeled to building technical artifacts, institutions, and skilled manpower to pursue this ambition.

This chapter describes how Indonesia, during the New Order regime (1966-1998), sought to institutionalize high technology as a means to accelerate development and modernization. In so doing, this paper relies on the approach of historical sociology to explain both the structure and agency shaping Indonesia's technological endeavor. Three levels of analysis will be presented in this paper. The first touches upon the ideological foundation and structure of power that underpinned the longevity of the New Order authoritarianism. Roles of individual actors, namely the engineers and political elites, are highlighted to show power relations that structured the political economy of technological development. The second level examines the organizing concept of technological development, namely "accelerated transformation" and how this concept became institutionalized. The last deals with the technical realization of the high technology vision, which failed to survive in the aftermath of the Asian crisis that struck Indonesia in 1997-1998. A few factors that caused the decline of the high technology ambition will be discussed briefly.

Rise of the New Order

Two decades after declaring its independence from the Dutch, who occupied the territory of what is Indonesia at present, Indonesian society was submerged into poverty. Political conflicts among the elites hindered the central government from being able to deliver what the people needed. Although successful in turning the whole country into one united nation, the first Indonesian president, Sukarno, had to deal with many difficulties in managing the new state with limited resources. His proclivities towards the Eastern bloc exacerbated the situation especially in the height of Cold War. By mid of 1960s, Sukarno's power abruptly dissolved after a silent coup that gave rise to the New Order regime led General Suharto.

Under Suharto's authoritarian leadership, Indonesia embarked upon economic development. The spread of development ideas in Indonesia initially began from the role of a group of economists of the University of Indonesia (FEUI) led by Widjojo Nitisastro. When power passed from Sukarno to Suharto in 1966, Suharto inherited an economic turbulence. Economic growth was practically 0%, while inflation reached an extremely high point, exceeding 500%. The percentage of the population living under the poverty line was 65%. Employing the neo-Keynesian paradigm, the New Order economists undertook a set of economic policies that included balancing the state budget, controlling money supply, reorganizing financial institutions, and most importantly, opening its national gates to welcome foreign investors. Bolstered by political stability, these policies performed so well that in two years Indonesian economy unprecedentedly experienced an economic growth of 10.9%, marking the beginning of the recovery phase.

According to political scientist William Liddle, the New Order regime is a classic example of a personal rule ubiquitous in many Third World countries. The shape of its power structure resembles a pyramid with Suharto at the top such that some minor turbulence at the top would produce major political effects at the bottom.[1] Yet, for these politi-

1 William Liddle, "Suharto's Indonesia: Personal Rule and Political Institutions" *Pacific Affairs* 85 (1985): 68-90.

cal effects to resonate to the lowest level of the social structure, a structural medium is required. Two underlying institutions of the New Order served such purposes. Each played a different yet equally important role in making Suharto's authoritarian regime work effectively. The first institution that strongly characterized the New Order as an authoritarian regime was the Indonesian Armed Forces (ABRI, now TNI).[2] Enabled by the doctrine dwifungsi stating the dual function of ABRI in defense and socio-political affairs, ABRI interfered with civilian affairs by occupying bureaucratic positions. In politics, ABRI attained unrivaled privileges by grasping free seats in the parliament without competition during election. Complementing ABRI's social and political roles was the policing function conducted under its doctrine of "Territorial Warfare". Such a doctrine was manifested in a network of territorial units, spanning the provincial level (Kodam) down to the sub-district level (Koramil), parallel with the civilian administration. The striking presence of ABRI in social and political affairs brought huge consequences to social and political life of the Indonesian society, building a system of total control over the population. Subsequently ABRI became a coercive organization that served to eliminate any possibility of the rise of civil disobedience against Suharto's leadership. The second pillar of Suharto's power was *Golongan Karya* (Functionary Group) or *Golkar* stemming from *Sekber Golkar* (the Join Secretariat of Functionary Groups) formed by military politicians in 1964 to counter the growing strength of the Communist party.[3] In 1971 *Golkar*

2 For a complete discussion of the politics of Indonesian army, see Harold Crouch, *The Army and Politics of Indonesia* (Ithaca, 1978).

3 An extensive historical account of Golkar is presented in David Reeve, *Golkar of Indonesia: an Alternative to the Party System* (Singapore, 1985).

was made the state party and since then had won every election held at five-year intervals. Relying on the military's territorial structure and a bureaucratic organization that reached deep down to the village level, *Golkar* maintained its presence in virtually every village across the country. Granted unrivaled resources, *Golkar* dominated Indonesian politics and served to provide electoral legitimacy to the New Order regime.

Conceptually, the New Order's development revolved around a modernization project that aimed at producing social changes following a postulate of Walt W. Rostow. According to this economic theorist, modernization consists of five stages of growth through which a society experiences transformation from traditional conditions to modern ones characterized by mass consumption.[4] As the Cold War era of the 1960s gave not much choice of modernization models–either capitalism or communism,[5] Rostow's modernization concept was more promising for American-oriented Third World governments, like the New Order. Brought about by American-educated economists and development planners, Rostow's idea permeated to Indonesian realms, spreading the capitalist dreams through the concept of take-off. This was explicitly inscribed in the New Order's twenty-five-year development goal, *masyarakat tinggal landas* (take-off society).

In 1969, the New Order started the first Five-Year Development Plan (Repelita) with a focus on infrastructure and agriculture. The New

4 Walt .W. Rostow, *The Stages of Economic Growth: A Non-Communist Manifesto* (Cambridge, 1964).

5 Suharto did not admit that capitalism was the path the New Order took. Rather, he argued that the New Order's development model was based on Pancasila, which combines socialism and capitalism.

Order's Trilogy of Development—growth, equality, and stability—was introduced to the public with more emphasis on the first and the third. Entering the 1970s, the economic growth paced up when international petroleum prices quadrupled due to the Israel-Arab War. Such a blessing in disguise conferred a massive windfall in revenue gains on Indonesian economy. As oil prices went down in the mid-1980s, the Repelita III was characterized by an economic transformation from agriculture-based to industry-based, emphasizing non-oil export commodities. The dawn of 1990s saw a total change in the Indonesian economy from that of the 1960s. The New Order has succeeded in transforming Indonesian's severely poor and backgward economy into a modern and developing one. From the end of 1960s to the mid of 1990s, the average economic growth stabilized at 6.5% per a year, thus trebling income per capita in just one generation. After years of being one of the largest rice importers, Indonesia achieved self-sufficiency in this crop in the mid-1980s. In 1991, industrial sectors' contribution to Growth Domestic Products (GDP) increased three times exceeding that of agricultural sectors, transforming the archipelagic nation a semi-industrialized country according to United Nations International Development Organization (UNIDO). Such an economic progress was ensued by an impressive development in social life. Only 10% of the population now lived under the poverty line, while the percentage of illiterate people remained 18.9 compared to 68.1 in the 1960s.[6] Amazed by these enormous achievements, Jeffrey E. Garten in his 1997 book included Indonesia as one of the ten most influen-

6 For a complete account of Indonesian economy since 1966, see Hall Hill, *The Indonesian Economy* (Cambridge, 2000).

tial economies in the world.[7]

It is important to note that technology was the very foundation of modernization in Indonesia. Since the first five-year development program, a variety of technology utilization programs were initiated to "conquer" the rich endowment of Indonesian lands. Agricultural mechanization enhanced the capability of farmers to make use of fertile soils in many islands of the country. Chemical substances were utilized to boost plant productivity in order to suffice needs of foodstuff. Using mapping and processing technology, forests were converted into timber industry, turning the earth's lungs into lucrative dollar makers. At the same time, gigantic dams were built to produce electricity indispensable for industrialization. Excavators and drill strings were operated to mine a variety of minerals e.g. gold, silver, copper, lead, iron, and the most of all, oil and gas. Every now and then, factories equipped with industrial machinery were erected , taking advantage of cheap labor to produce a myriad of manufactured goods. Human body was even subject to technological interference. With the use of birth control devices, sex was "regulated" for the sake of development through Family Plan Program.[8] "Politics have entered the bedroom," a feminist activist once cynically commented. The entire conquest of nature was ultimately expressed in the collection of physical edifices, concentrated mostly in the metropolitan Jakarta that

7 Jeffrey E. Garten, *The Big Ten: the Big Emerging Market and How They Will Change Our Lives*. (New York, 1997).

8 Unlike Sukarno who was proud of the vastness of Indonesian population, in Suharto's regime large population was a problem to be overcome. In 1989, Suharto received Population Award from the United Nations for the success of Family Plan Program in lowering Indonesia's birth rate.

symbolized the success of the New Order. Smoothly paved highways with imported cars running on them, glossy glass walls of steel skyscrapers, beautiful monuments built to entice , and dazzling colorful lights on streets all celebrated and represented the dawn of a new era of Indonesian modernity.

Behind the New Order's cultural and natural transformation of the Indonesian landscape was a technology imagination fueled by a postcolonial modernity narrative. This imagination rendered technology something more than just a material production, but as a fulfillment of the desire for prosperity, prestige, and ultimately power. At this point, the New Order constructed 'Indonesia' as a technological nation, embedding technology as part of its national culture. Parallel to the nationalist ideology, technology was now a unifying medium of a widely diverse nation composed by social groups culturally and geographically separated one another. It is the matrix between the broadened meaning of technology and the New Order's ideological aims that unleashed social, political, and cultural forces for the emergence of technological nationalism.

The Engineers

The incorporation of high technology into Indonesian development during the New Order era was triggered by the presence of a group of elite engineers led by Bacharuddin Jusuf Habibie, who happened to know Suharto long before the general came to power as the leader of the New Order. After completing a doctoral program at the Technical University at Aachen in 1965, Habibie worked for the German aircraft manufacturer Messerschmitt-Boelkow-Blohm (MBB) until he attained a position of vice president and director for technology application in 1974 (Makka, 1989). By that time, Suharto had succeeded in consolidating his power, placing himself at the pinnacle of the political structure. Being passionate about technology he saw as instrumental for Indonesia's transformation into an industrial economy, Suharto launched a national development program. In need of assistance from an expert with knowledge in high technology, Suharto summoned his old friend in Germany to repatriate. Habibie felt excited about Suharto's invitation and immediately prepared for a homecoming. In January 1974, Habibie met Suharto in the Presidential Palace, a reunion that led to the materialization of Indonesia's high technology development. Since then, Suharto and Habibie created a relationship which benefited each other. On one side, Habibie leveraged on Suharto's political dominance to realize his technological fantasy while on the other, Suharto relied on Habibie's scientific credentials to pursue his regime's interests in high technology. This symbiotic mutual-power relationship in turn produced centrifugal effects on the New Order's politics, especially in the 1990s when the New Order reached its height.[9]

Habibie started his career in the New Order by joining the state-owned oil company Pertamina in which, for two years, he led the Advanced Technology Division. Assisted by a few Indonesian engineers he had hired during his tenure at MBB, Habibie formulated a plan to devel-

9 Sulfikar Amir, "Symbolic Power in a Technocratic Regime: The Reign of B. J. Habibie in New Order Indonesia," *Sojourn: Journal of Social Issues in Southeast Asia* 22(1) (April 2007): 83-106.

op a modern aircraft manufacturing industry, thus realizing his long-time dream. In 1976, with the enormous funding support from state-owned oil company Pertamina, Habibie founded Indonesian Aircraft Industry (IPTN) with himself as the President Director. Two years later, Suharto named Habibie the Minister for Research and Technology and Head of Agency for the Assessment and Application of Technology (BPPT). For twenty years, Habibie occupied these top positions making him the New Order's longest serving minister.

The engineers were not the only technocratic group that had joined Suharto's administration. From the outset, the New Order's economic policy had been designed and planned by a group of economists, led by Widjojo Nitisastro, who subscribed to a developmental paradigm emphasizing comparative advantages as opposed to competitive ones promoted by the engineers. The contrasting views of the engineers and the economists consequently resulted in a rivalry of technocracy, which lasted throughout the whole period of the New Order rule. The triumph of the engineers and the decline of the economists reached a climax when Suharto announced the composition of the Sixth Development Cabinet in March 1993. A number of ministerial positions usually held by Widjojo's protégés were now shared with other groups, most notably the engineers. The rise of the engineers is related to changes in the New Order's agenda of long-term development plans. Following Rostow's theory of stages of growth, the economists had devised a long-term development plan conceived on a twenty-five year basis. Starting in 1993, the Sixth Development Cabinet was intended to celebrate the second twenty-five years of this development plan, a phase known as *Pembangunan Jangka Panjang Tahap Kedua* (PJPT 2). Equally important to note is the epistemological boundary that distinguishes the engineers from the economists as regards to their technocratic paradigms. It lies in one ideal condition that existed only in the engineers' vocabulary, namely *mandiri*. This word is all over the discourses of technological development found in almost every text of the New Order's long-term development plan. *Mandiri* literally means "independent" or "autonomous". Such a word, absent in the economists' rational definition of the economy, emphasizes a set of political, ideological, and cultural objectives. As it permeates the technocratic paradigm of the engineers, the concept of mandiri bears a powerful impetus to pursue technology as a form of independence. This is clearly expressed in the way Habibie linked nationalism to economy.

> [N]ationalism is much broader than the necessary conditions of political independence. In the economy, nationalism refers to the capability of producing goods and services for our own needs...Therefore, mastering and developing technology are very important. Without this, our rich natural endowment would never be under our own control.[10]

The concept of *mandiri* is rooted in what I call a "culture of production" that deeply characterizes engineering practice. The culture of production revolves around manipulation, i.e. to transform one sort of energy, material, or condition into something technically useful. From this point of view, technology is strongly associated with a state of self-governance, self-sufficiency, and self-determination. Thus, the material-

10 Bacharuddin J. Habibie, *Ilmu Pengetahuan, Teknologi, dan Pembangunan Bangsa [Science, Technology, and Development for the Nation]* (Jakarta, 1995).

ization of technology in economic development becomes an ingredient in nationalist claims that fueled the engineers' technocratic worldview. This eventually turned policymaking into an arena of contestation about modernity. While the economists identified modern conditions primarily as those of growth and wealth creation, the engineers proposed that modernity was a condition of being technologically independent. In the end, this conflation of the rhetoric of nationalism and technocratic epistemology conferered enormous power effect on Habibie and his engineer colleagues. They took control of key bureaucratic institutions and promoted the operation of IPTN as the symbol of technological independence of the nation.

Accelerated Transformation

A close acquaintance to Suharto, Habibie and his engineers group had access to nearly unlimited state resources to realize the dream of Indonesian high technology that he shared with Suharto. For over twenty years, Habibie and his entourage dominated the discourse of technology development in which he argued that the development of high technology was the only option a country like Indonesia should pursue to catch up with industrially advanced nations.

Habibie's justification for the pursuit of high technology lies in the notion of accelerated transformation. This notion is partly inspired by the experiences of East Asian Newly Industrialized Countries, namely South Korea, Taiwan, Hong Kong, and Singapore that succeeded to achieve high economic growth through extensive utilization of technology in industrialization process. It took about 30 years for this group of countries to transform their economies from agriculture-dependent to industrial-based ones. Habibie had convinced Suharto that despite its complexity as a multicultural society and a sheer number of population, Indonesia would be able to accelerate socio-economic transformation to follow what other Asian nations have accomplished.

Conceptually, Habibie's idea of accelerated transformation is encapsulated in his phrase *berawal dari akhir, berakhir di awal* (starting from the end, ending at the start). This refers to a reversion of industrialization process consisting of four steps of transformation.[11] The first step is the use of technology to produce existing products that leads to added value creation. This involves transfer of technology from foreign countries initially through license-based manufacturing activity. The goal of this stage is to familiarize local engineers and technicians with the complexity of technological processes. Through this, people acquire basic know-how and experience in operating complicated technologies.

The second step is characterized by new product development based on existing technology. This step involves the creativity of local engineers in designing new products based on technology adapted from foreign sources. Following this step is the development of technology, which encompasses not only a totally new product, but also new technical systems. This is the point where local engineers indigenously develop an original technology. Once this step is achieved, dependence on foreign technology can, in principle, be eliminated. The whole process culminates the final step -conducting basic research. This step is achieved by produc-

11 Ibid., 211-7.

ing new knowledge in scientific laboratories.

The four-step transformation that functioned as the bedrock of IPTN under Habibie's rules was linked to social change and modernization. Habibie built this link by starting from the teleology of modernity that shaped the New Order development agendas. Taking Western social history as the platform, this teleology assumes that every society is geared towards modernity in which the institutionalization of economic development and complex social systems takes place. The development of societies in Western Europe and North America whose economies have reached sustained wealth reflect successful examples of how the teleology of modernity fueled sustainable welfare. Habibie believed that key to this tranformation was the input of technology. Drawn from his life experience during the post-war German economic miracle, Habibie saw that social evolution is a process that could be deliberately accelerated. Learning from experiences of developed societies, Habibie prescribed a shortcut trajectory to accelerate processes of social evolution through planned, hi-tech based industrialization. Central to this mechanism was the four-step transformation with IPTN as a model that would drive the whole process of social transformation moving from traditional conditions to modern ones. Under such a framework, technology has a twofold function: as an engine of growth and an agent of change. While simultaneously creating economic welfare, technology stimulates social and cultural processes in society moving towards modernity. Even more striking from Habibie's theory is the assertion that the accelerated evolution was subject to prediction and control. As Habibie put it:

> Accelerated evolution is entirely different from the concept of leapfrog-

> ging. Leapfrogging is random and unpredictable. Accelerated evolution is not random because its motion can be controlled and predicted. This means risks and costs of transformation can be reduced.[12]

From the way Habibie depicted the IPTN as engine of social transformation, it seems that Habibie saw social transformation analogous to an engineering process in which society is likened to a mechanical system consisting of interrelated elements. Viewing social process through engineering lens, Habibie placed technological change as the central mechanism that would drive the social system to function to achieve the new creation of a modern society. Habibie assumed that technology has embedded in it modern values from which society could learn, thereby adapting itself to the operational conditions that technology requires. In a nutshell, it is the introduction of new technology that drives social change.

Building Technological Institutions

The actions of Habibie and his supporters shaped the edifice of scientific and technological institutions so that they were totally under the control of Habibie himself. It did not take long for Habibie to expand the State Ministry for Research and Technology to a bureaucratic empire of science and technology.

The force of Habibie's technocratic dominance in technology policy

12 Habibie, 53.

ultimately stemmed from the bureaucratic structures placed under the full authority of the State Minister for Research and Technology. There were six non-departmental research institutions whose activities were under unassailable control of Habibie. These institutions included the Indonesian Institute of Sciences (LIPI), Agency for Mapping and Surveys (BAKOSURTANAL), National Institute of Aeronautic and Space (LAPAN), Agency for the Assessment and Application of Technology (BPPT), Central Bureau of Statistics (BPS), and National Nuclear Energy Agency (BATAN). Completing the tasks of these research institutions was Research Center for Science and Technology Development (PUSPIPTEK) located in Serpong, in the outskirts of Jakarta. This technoscience park houses a number of cutting-edge R&D laboratories where scientists and engineers from the aforementioned institutions conduct research activities. It should be noted that all research institutions under Habibie did not only constitute the entire research activity of the government. Other ministries e.g. transportation, agriculture, health, industry and trade, etc. had their own research and development division. But many of these research institutes were poorly funded. Their scientific infrastructures lagged behind those of laboratories in PUSPIPTEK, for example.

Of all research institutions under the jurisdiction of the State Minister for Research and Technology, the most important one to note was Agency for the Assessment and Application of Technology (BPPT) also headed by Habibie. Since its inception, BPPT has been given tasks which cover not only coordinating research activities, but more importantly the task of micro-economic planning, functioning as the counterpart and rival of BAPPENAS in charge of macro-economic planning.[13] While the role of BAPPENAS is limited to policy formulation of macro economy, BPPT holds authority that goes beyond planning. In addition to policy formulation, its powerful role lies in the capacity to coordinate research activities, to conduct technological research and assessment, and to provide research training for young scientists and engineers.[14] With hundreds of PhDs, the BPPT administers several scientific laboratories for research in engineering design, infrastructure, biotechnology, energy, microelectronics, and material. Most researchers obtained degrees abroad through study programs such as the Overseas Fellowship Program and the Science and Technology for Industrial Development (STAID), both drawn from soft loans from the World Bank and Japan's OECF (Overseas Economic Cooperation Fund).[15] With bureaucratic capacity broader than that of BAPPENAS, the strategic function of the BPPT, as political scientist Takashi Shiraishi notes, emanated from turning "assessment and application of technology into bureaucratic magic word"[16] that allowed this agency to engage in any technology-related development program. Because every government project to some extent contains aspects of

13 Suharto et al., *Pikiran, Ucapan, dan Tindakan Saya: Otobiografi [My Thought, Words, and Deeds: an Autobiography]*. (Jakarta, 1989).

14 Rony M. Bishry, and Murman Hidayat, "The Role of BPPT in Indonesia's Technological Challenge" in *Indonesia's Technological Challenge*, eds., Hal Hill and Thee Kian Wie (Singapore: 1998).

15 Notwithstanding the prestige of BPPT, a vast majority of BPPT qualified researchers are poorly paid because of their status as government employees. Consequently, they often do moonlighting outside as engineering consultant for private business. This inevitably affects the productivity of BPPT.

16 Takashi Shiraishi, "Rewiring the Indonesian State" in *Making Indonesia: Essays on Modern Indonesia in Honor of George Mct. Kahin*, eds., Ruth McVey Daniel M. Lev, (Ithaca: 1995).

technology, such flexibility gave the BPPT extensive opportunities to involve itself in many projects in the fields of basic needs, natural resources and energy, industrialization, defense, and social and economic development. Thus, naturally the BPPT could participate in various projects from appropriate technology for transmigrants in West Papua to nuclear reactor installation in PUSPIPTEK. The BPPT is also involved in several government councils such as National Telecommunication Council and the National Council for Work Safety, and inter departmental committees such as the Automotive Industry and the Second Digital Switching System. Most of all, the BPPT representatives are included in a coordinating committee that approves every government contract.[17]

Side-by-side the BPPT in enlarging the bureaucratic encroachment of Habibie and his group was the Agency for Strategic Industries Management (BPIS). This agency originated from the secretariat of the ministerial Council on Strategic Industries (DPIS) within BPPT in 1983. Composed of seven ministers with the State Minister for Research and Technology as the chair, DPIS was responsible of managing eight state-owned companies. The status of DPIS ascended when in 1989 Suharto formed the Agency for Strategic Industries Management (BPIS) while granting the participating ministers in the DPIS a task of policy design to be implemented by BPIS. At the point, the membership of the BPIS enlarged to nine ministers–Industry, Defense and Security, Transportation, Finance, Post and Telecommunication, State Secretary, State Minister for National Development Planning, and Commander-in-Chief of

17 François. Raillon, *Indonesia 2000: the Industrial and Technological Challenge* (Paris; Jakarta, 1990).

the Armed Forces–and the number of companies under the supervision of BPIS grew to ten including IPTN, PAL (shipbuilding), Krakatau Steel (iron and steel products), PINDAD (small arms), Dahana (explosives), INTI (telecommunication), INKA (rolling stock), BBI (machine-tools), Barata (heavy equipment) and LEN (microelectronics).

The presence of BPIS, however, was surrounded by controversy. Before this agency was created, those strategic industries belonged to technical departments i.e. Transportation (INKA), Post and Telecommunication (INTI), Industry (BBI and Barata). Two of them were in the hands of the military i.e. PAL (the Navy) and PINDAD (the Army). LEN was the only one coming from a research institute LIPI. With status of state-owned companies, these large corporations were no more than cash cows serving the interests of well-positioned bureaucrats and military officials. When Habibie pooled all strategic industries under his jurisdiction with the favor of Suharto, feelings of discontent spread among some ministers and the Armed Forces generals towards Habibie. These tensions escalated because Habibie had obtained not only the chair position of BPIS, but also the directorship of IPTN, PAL, and PINDAD. Nevertheless, Habibie's position remained strong.

The uniqueness of BPIS came from the powerful concept "strategic industries." The term "strategic industries" has two meanings. First, it refers to state industries that produce goods with high technological contents. Second, strategic industries are defined as those playing a special role in supporting national integrity, sovereignty, and defense. The conflation of these two meanings gave Habibie and the engineer group tremendous power to control large-scale industries that employed no less than 43,000 workers with total assets in 1999 amounting to US $16 billion. Despite its status as a state agency, BPIS practically was a holding company. By holding the chair position of BPIS along with the directorships of three industries under this agency, Habibie evolved into a high-level businessman. This is the position that the economists did not have a chance to attain.

Conceptually, the core mission of BPIS was to function as a venue for implementing technology development that private sectors were not able to pursue. Hence, there was a strong link at work between BPIS and BPPT. While BPPT was supposed to generate inventions and innovations, BPIS was the outlet of production and commercialization of what BPPT had produced. The goal of placing BPPT and BPIS in Habibie's hands was to make synergy between scientific research and development and industrial production. Five years after the establishment of BPIS, it turned out that the BPIS failed to achieve synergy. Despite one or two successful projects of BPIS such as the national car project, overall the management of BPIS was still poor and inefficient. As one former BPIS official pointed out, the problem of BPIS lied in the centralization of all decisions in Habibie's hands.

Producing High Technology: the Aircraft Industry

The New Order's ambition to produce high technologies was materialized in a number of projects that ranged from telecommunication, weaponry, transportation, and satellites. However, the most prestigious was the Indonesian Aircraft Industry (IPTN), which received more attention from Suharto himself. Located in the city of Bandung, IPTN was founded in 1976. By 1995, it was employing more than 16,000 people of whom hundreds were Indonesia's best scientists and engineers, with doctoral degrees from prestigious universities around the world. The company produced aircraft components and a variety of helicopters and propeller-driven airplanes. Covering an area of 79.3 hectares of buildings near the Husain Sastranegara airport, IPTN was equipped with advanced manufacturing technology and a real-time computer system for conducting state-of-the-art aeronautical research, design, and production activities, along with remarkable maintenance facilities built to serve the needs of domestic airlines. Over the course of two decades, the New Order government invested more than US $1.2 billion in IPTN, an enormous amount that indicated a tenacious commitment of the government to foster this emerging high technology industry.

IPTN operations began with agreements with MBB and Construccione´s Aeronauticas, S.A. (CASA) of Spain. These two European companies provided technological assistance to IPTN during its infancy. As a start-up, IPTN produced under license MBB's BO-105 helicopters and CASA's 12-passenger C-212 Aviocar. It took 3 years for IPTN technicians to learn how to construct an aircraft down to its smallest parts. This process required both technical and administrative skills, for every part had to be drawn and documented. During the first decade, IPTN grew rapidly in terms of employee numbers and projects. Several joint ventures with Western corporations were signed. For example, IPTN and French Aerospatiale agreed to produce the PUMA SA 330; IPTN and Bell Helicopter Textron manufactured 100 Bell-412 helicopters. In 1986, IPTN succeeding in getting an order from General Dynamics to manufacture F-16 components.

In 1979, IPTN and CASA agreed to jointly develop a new propeller aircraft called CN235. This 35-seat aircraft was designed for medium-range distance based on the US FAR Part 25. It cost US$ 20 million, a cost shared equally by IPTN and CASA through ownership of Aircraft Technologies Corporation (AIRTEC) based in Madrid. During the project, IPTN engineers flew back and forth to Spain to learn from and work together with their counterparts at CASA. The CN235 was designed to suit two different purposes. For Indonesian purposes, IPTN wanted to use it in military operations in remote areas. It was intended to replace the C130 Hercules, which was used extensively by the Indonesian military.

One year after the completion of CN235 project, IPTN embarked on another project. This time it proceeded alone, with no foreign counterpart–a risky endeavor given that IPTN was a relative rookie in the business. The risk of failure aside, however, Habibie believed the time had come for IPTN to develop its own technology independently, and he felt certain IPTN engineers were capable of carrying out such a mission. In addition, he wanted IPTN to build a commercial aircraft that would be competitive in the civilian airline industry, as building solely for the military market did not produce enough profit. In 1987, a small team of IPTN engineers conducted a survey of the emerging market in regional flights with a range of 800 miles. The team learned that many of the Fokker 27 airplanes used by Indonesian airlines were about to be phased out. A moderate estimate suggested 400 mid-range airplanes, with possibly a higher number in foreign markets. In the early stage, the new project sought to design a 30-seat aircraft, hence the title N230. Later, the project was renamed N25011 after further study revealed that the market wanted a 50-seat aircraft. At the 1989 Paris Air Show, Habibie publicly announced the N250 project to the international aviation community.

The N250 is a propeller aircraft that cruises at speeds up to 330 knots, the fastest propeller airplane in the subsonic class. It relies on a fly-by-wire flight control system that provides electrically controlled hydraulic service for both primary and secondary control surfaces of an airplane. The N250's fly-by-wire covers three axes–directional, lateral, and longitudinal–a great innovation considering similar systems covered only one or two axes. IPTN engineers later extended the N250's structure to accommodate 70 seats without additional engine power, making it more attractive in the market. Habibie was confident that the N250 would be competitive in the world market. To penetrate the North American market, IPTN opened a branch office in Seattle. It also planned to build a manufacturing plant in Mobile, Alabama. The superiority of the N250's technical features became a source of pride for the whole coun-

Figure 1. The N250's first flight. [Source: IPTN Document]

try. Claimed to be entirely created by Indonesian engineers, the N250 marked what Habibie called the "stage of technological independence" which helped to IPTN's capability to master sophisticated technologies and move forward in the development of new ones. The N250 was the symbol of technological nationalism that Habibie and his engineers at IPTN had relentlessly advocated and envisioned.

On August 10, 1995, the N250 made its maiden flight before Suharto, Habibie, and the entire cabinet of the New Order government. This event marked a historic moment in Indonesia's history of technology that is hitherto celebrated every year as the Technology Reawakening Day. The euphoria of the N250's successful flight test gave a tremendous boost to the reputation of Habibie and his group. It vindicated his high technology vision, rescuing it from skepticism and cynicism.

The N250 was not the climax of the New Order's technological ambition. The N250 was the third step in his concept of four-step transformation. There was one more step he needed to take to finish his job. Harnessing the euphoria of the N250's successful maiden flight, in the press conference held after the N250 flew Habibie announced a new project of developing a 130-seater jet airplane called N2130. Habibie's oldest son, Germany-born and educated Dr. Ilham Akbar Habibie, was named the director of the even more ambitious enterprise.

The development cost of this jet airplane was estimated to be US $2 billions. This time Habibie was aware that he could no longer rely on the government funds alone. To finance the project, Suharto had prepared a seemingly bizarre plan. A company named DSTP standing for *Dua Satu Tiga Puluh* or Two One Thirty was established with a mission of collecting funds from the entire Indonesian people. Suharto assigned Saadillah

Mursjid, then cabinet secretariat minister, as the president director of the DSTP. Suharto assumed that if every Indonesian bought DSTP's shares, then sufficient funds would be available to finish the project.[18]

Suharto traveled around the country urging the people, even farmers in rural areas, to participate in the N2130 project. Suharto called this collective action as *gotongroyong*, an allegedly indigenous concept in Indonesia culture as Sukarno claimed to be the tenet of Pancasila. He imagined that someday farmers would look at the N2130 airplane flying over them and proudly said, "Look, I have a contribution to that airplane."[19] One can find an irony in this imagination. Indonesian farmers had long been deprived and that it was highly unlikely that a prestigious jet airplane project would help them improve their economic life. Yet, farmers were not alone in being subjects of such a coercive fantasy. Using the bureaucracy network, the New Order government obliged all government employees to purchase DSTP's shares. Some of them indeed had no objection to contributing. But the fact that a group of poorly paid schoolteachers were charged DSTP shares in their monthly salaries without their consent was terribly upsetting.[20] Once again, a technological nationalist project began and Suharto encouraged Indonesian people to show their nationalistic spirit by supporting the N2130 project.

---

18 See Saadillah. Mursjid "The Funding of PT DSTP, a High Technology Project: Lofty Goals, Defined Task." in *Indonesia's Technological Challenge*, eds., Hall Hill and Kian Wie Thee. (Singapore, 1998).

19 Interview with former vice-chair of BPIS Giri Suseno, 8 June 2004.

20 Interview with Indonesian Teacher Union president Basyuni Suriamiharja. Tempo Online. 24 September 1997.

The Force of Globalization

In July 1997, the Asian financial crises that originally broke out in East Asia reached Southeast Asia. Two years after Indonesia celebrated the success of the N250's maiden flight, the situation turned upside down. Optimism shown in the beginning of 1997 was washed out by an unpredictable crisis. The financial contagion soon spread to Indonesia. In July 1997 the value of rupiah fell from 2,400 to 3,600 to dollar. Only a few months later, the rupiah experienced a free fall to an exchange rate of 9,500 to dollar.

In March 1998, amidst the economic turmoil, Suharto moved on to his seventh term as President, and B.J. Habibie was named vice president. Desperately seeking financial aid from the IMF, Suharto signed an agreement to phase out subsidies of basic commodities such as fuel, electricity, and public transportation. This policy was greeted with public anger. Soon students burst out in streets protesting the policy while demanding economic and political reforms. Suharto, who seemed exhausted by the crisis, responded by sending security apparatus against student demonstrations, which resulted in bloody confrontations. In an incident on May 15, 1998, four students of Trisakti University were gunned down by the police. The death of these students escalated the tension to an extreme. During May 16 and 17, streets riots exploded in a number of large cities, but Jakarta suffered the worst damage. The New Order was near collapse. In the morning of May 21, Suharto appeared on national television announcing his resignation, leaving the country in political chaos. Under terms of the constitution, Habibie was sworn in as the third president of Indonesia, eventually succeeding the master he had long served.

For seventeen months, Habibie's transitional administration managed to deal with multi-dimensional crises. Yet, in the end he failed to sustain his presidency.

A number of analyses can help explain how Indonesia dramatically changed overnight from an Asian "miracle" to a country with thousands of problems. Economic analyses drawn from external factors mostly blamed unstable financial markets and the mishandling of international financial institutions. Internal factor analyses pointed to the problems of macroeconomic policy weaknesses, domestic financial sectors, and crony-capitalism. The latter interpretations coincided with political analyses that emphasized the New Order's political institutions, corrupt and devoid of democracy, as the main cause of the fall of Suharto's regime.

The cause of the crisis sparked a heated debate among analysts. What is apparent from this crisis is that it entailed far-reaching implications for the IPTN. The shift of power altered the destiny of this once prominent focus of national pride. After years of being spoiled with almost unlimited financial resources, the arrival of IMF to help the Suharto government muddle through the crisis inexorably impacted the IPTN. Witnessed by the IMF managing director Michael Camdessus, Suharto signed a memorandum of economic and financial policies on January 15, 1998. One point in the memo explicitly stated that the government would cease subsidies for the IPTN. As Camdessus pointed out in a press conference, the withdrawal of the IPTN subsidy was based on a consideration that public spending must be limited to those of vital importance to the country.

For the economists long critical to Habibie's hi-tech programs, cutting the IPTN loose from the government support was a rational decision given the sizable amount of public funds IPTN had absorbed. But Habibie and his group of technological nationalists were suspicious of the IMF's ban on the IPTN funding. There was a shared conviction among Habibie and his group that a conspiracy to bring down the IPTN was underneath the enforced agreement. Rahardi Ramelan, for instance, believed that the IMF memorandum was used to protect the interest of American aviation industry.[21]

However one might interpret these events that even Suharto and his last cabinet could not do anything to save IPTN from drastic cuts. After a new government was formed through a democratic election in 1999, the subsidy for IPTN was abruptly withdrawn. Consequently, all the ongoing projects of IPTN encountered difficulties as the company had to deal with enormous financial problems, including debts and unpaid salaries. The $2 billion N2130 jet airplane project led by Habibie's oldest son was terminated as its financing company, DSTP, was closed down by the government. In a similar situation, the strategic industries agency BPIS through which Habibie controlled ten state-owned companies could not survive political disturbance. It was finally dismissed in August 1998. As with the N250 project, this symbol of Indonesia's technological grandeur stagnated in its third prototype production. Though the second prototype flew in February 1996, it failed to earn an FAA airworthiness certificate due to poor documentation. Hence, this product that carried great national ambitions never reached the market.

21 Interview with Rahardi Ramelan, 7 July 2003.

Conclusion

Despite twenty years of extensive efforts the New Order regime had invested in building techno scientific infrastructure and institutions, Indonesia remains left behind by Asian industrialized nations in terms of techno-economic performances. The fiasco of the New Order's ambitious projects conceptualized by Habibie-led engineers group tragically marks the end of the regime's rule as well as the decline of technological nationalism in Indonesia at least for a moment. What lessons can we learn from Indonesia's experience in trying to catch up with technologically advanced states through the accelerated transformation approach?

There are two insights that can be drawn from the case of high technology development illustrated throughout this paper. The first deals with the rationality behind the New Order's tenacious attempt to undertake accelerated transformation relying on high technology. It is quite obvious that the whole enterprise of constructing high technologies is tied to an imagination of Western modernity for which the New Order elites aspired. One can sense a very strong notion of technological determinism that informed the New Order engineer technocrats to go to the developmental direction that emphasizes the role of technology as the driving force of socio-economic transformation. This, however, does not come without consequences. The concept of accelerated transformation is part of the New Order authoritarian rule that sought to transform society through undemocratic means. The imposition of such a vision into a complex society like Indonesia resulted in an ineffective transformation and only produced elitist outcomes. What is more important to note is that despite the successful outputs of technological innovation exemplified in the N250, the hi-tech development envisioned by Habibie and his technocratic group did not come with adequate institutional supports from non-technological sectors such as trade, finance, and education. As a result, this vision failed to penetrate other sectors and remained focused on one specific domain in development policy, namely science and technology.

The second insight relates to the relationship between technology and politics. Scholars of Science and Technology Studies (STS) have provided ample examples that demonstrate the interplay between technology and politics. The history of the New Order's technological endeavor vividly shows such an interconnection in which politics is what has fueled very much the development of high technology in Indonesia. In fact, the entire edifice of technological institutions and artifacts constructed by the engineers was made possible by power relations that underpinned the New Order authoritarianism.

While the New Order's high technology development was born to politics, it is the same politics that rendered its demise. As the high technology vision was tightly embedded in the power relations of the New Order regime, it suffered together with the collapse of the regime. Suharto's power decline correspondingly saw the painful dismantle of Habibie's technological projects undertaken by the post-Suharto administration. It is very clear that the hi-tech vision failed to survive political changes that swept out Suharto's developmental authoritarianism.

Development in Science and Technology of South Korea During the Cold War

Focusing on the US Policy Toward South Korea*

Tae Gyun Park

Introduction

South Korea's economic growth has often been studied as a model of the developmental state theory. Indeed, the speed and effectiveness of Korea's case are exceptional compared to those of any other developing countries. Recently many researchers in history of science have examined why and how South Korea was able to achieve scientific and technological development simultaneously with this economic growth. What triggered such a rapid development of science and technology?

Scholars abroad have focused on several points overall. First, they stress that the development of science and technology was achieved in a top-down manner under the leadership of the government [1] In particu-

* This paper is written under a project, "The 120 History of Electricity in Korea," funded by the National Research Foundation of Korea. (NRF Project No. 2009-0084888) This

lar, they point to the Park Chung Hee administration as the first regime to emphasize the significance of science and technology policy, which it promoted by measures such as providing subsidies to the industrialization strategy. In fact, the science and technology policy under the Park government was deeply connected with special development strategies for the heavy chemical industry of the 1970s.[2]

Korean researchers in history of science emphasize the changes that occurred in the late 1960s. They point out that both the an administration for science and technology and Korea Institute of Science and Technology (KIST) were established during this period, marking the beginning of concentrated efforts by the government to formulate a science and technology policy. Such changes also illustrate that South Korean scientists' demands for the promotion of science and technology had also built up by then.[3] Along with a generational change of science and technology policy makers, President Park intended to use scientific and technological development as a political and economic tool, like another fascist leader.[4] The main interest of this study, however, is not

---

paper is a revised version of which was published in *Korea Journal* Vol. 52, No. 1, 2012.

1 Joel Ross Campbell, "Creating Technology Capacity: The Changing Role of the Korean State Since the Third Republic," PhD dissertation, University of Miami, Miami, 1991; Bang-Soon L. Yoon, "State Power and public R&D in Korea: A case study of the Korea Institute of Science and Technology," PhD dissertation, University of Hawaii, Honolulu, 1992.

2 This argument created another story of President Park Chung Hee as a pioneer and leader to promote science and technology. Most scholars of this tendency chiefly rely on memoirs of former economic bureaucrats like O Won-Chul and Kim Jeong Ryeom.

3 Moon, Manyong, "1960Nyeondae Gwahakgisul Bum: Hangugui Hyeondaejeok Gwahakgisulchejeui Hyeongseong" ["The Science and Technology Boom in 1960s: The Formation of Science and Technology System in Korea,"], *Journal of the Korean History of Science Society*, 29-1 (2007): 69-98.

4 Kim, Geun Bae, "Gwahakgisuripgugui Haebu-do : 1960Nyeondae Gwahakgisul Ji-

in the internal dynamics of South Korea during the period but in the external conditions that had a strong impact on domestic politics. The issue is closely linked to a critical assessment of the developmental state theories. A decisive limitation of the theory is that it overlooks the important role played by the transfer of capital, knowledge, and technology from outside in the developing countries.[5] The main argument of this thesis is that external factors played a more decisive role in the development of science and technology than internal dynamics. It is important to consider that Korea was a divided country surrounded by superpowers - Japan and China – and thus at the frontline of the Cold War. In these circumstances, the direction of Korea's development as well as drawback in science and technology was determined by the conditions of the Cold War. In the following sections, I will examine how the Cold War drove the development of Korea's science and technology in a certain direction, from 1945 to the late 1970s.

Selected Scientists under the USAMGIK

The historical study of modern science and technology was import-

---

hyeong" ["An Anatomical Chart of Establishing the Scientific and Technological State: The Topography of Science and Technology in South Korea in the 1960s,"] *Critical Review of History*, 65 (2008): 236-261.

5 Jim Glassman and Choi, Young Jin, "Chaebol and Developmentalism State: Geopolitical Economics of the Cold War and Disciplines of the Capital," Presentation Paper, The 3rd International Symposium of KIKS, (Seoul: Seoul National University, 2010); Park, Tae Gyun, "Park Chung Hee Jeongbu Sigireul Tonghae Bon Baljeonguk-ga Damnone Daehan Bipanjeok Siron", ["Reassessing the Developmental State Theory through Park Era,"] *Quarterly Review of Korean History: Past and Present*, 74 (2009).

ed to Korea in the 18th century by intellectuals who were introduced to Western philosophy through their interactions with Qing China. However, it was not easy for Korean scholars to popularize new science and technology until the mid-19th century in Joseon, since the Confucianism as an ideological tool was too strong to be replaced by another idea.

Although western missionaries in the late 19th century played a role to spread education of modern science, fundamental development of modern science technology was started through Japan after its colonization of the peninsula like any other colonies before the World War II. Thus, at the moment of the demise of the Japanese Empire in 1945, Korea's science and technology remained deeply influenced by Japan.

Shortly after independence from Japan, Lee Tae-Gyu, Kim Bong-Jip, An Dong-Hyeok, Kim Dong-Il and others formed a society of professors in science and technology. Most members of the society, which was led by Lee Tae-Gyu, came from the College of Science and Engineering, Keijo Imperial University. They considered science and technology as one of founding stones in the restoration of the Korean state and submitted to the U.S. Army Military Government in Korea (USAMGIK) a plan for promoting education of the science and technology and for establishing the Ministry of Science and Education. Their suggestions were partly reflected in the policies adopted by the Education Department of the USAMGIK.[6]

6 Lee Tae-Gyu received his doctorate from Kyoto Imperial University and worked for the university as a professor until 1945. After returning in November 1945, he was appointed as a dean at the College of Science and Engineering at Keijo Imperial University, which joined Seoul National University in 1946. Additionally, he served for the USAMGIK as a committee member for high education.

USAMGIK received advice from several specialists in science and technology, who were the key figures in devising the policy of "Promoting Education in Science" in 1945-1946: Lee Hi-Jun (graduated from the Civil Engineering Department of Kyoto Imperial University in 1926, worked as an engineer in the Ministry of Home Affairs of the Japanese Government General in Korea, executive director of Samcheok, Inc. in the district of Kanto, Manchuria, and financial officer of Planning Administration), Jeong Mun-Ki (graduated from the Fisheries Department of Tokyo Imperial University in 1929, principal of Fisheries Experiment Station, dean of Busan Fisheries College), Jo Baek-Hyeon (graduated from the Agricultural Chemistry Department of Kyushu Imperial University in 1925, engineer of the Agricultural Station, professor of Suwon Agriculture and Forestry School for Higher Education, dean of Suwon Agriculture and Forestry College), Kim No-Su (graduated from the Machinery Department of Waseda University in 1939, engineer of Railroads Bureau, chief of the manufacture section in Department of Transportation), An Dong-Hyeok (graduated from the Department of Applied Chemistry of Kyushu Imperial University in 1929, engineer of the Central Test Institutee, professor of Keijo Technical College, director of Central Industrial Research Institute), Lee Tae-Gyu, and Yun Il-Seon (graduated from the Medical College of Kyoto Imperial University in 1923, professor of Severance Medical College, head of the Department of Medicine at Keijo Imperial University).[7] The specialists in scientific technology of the time stressed that education in science and technology will be crucial in building the new state and will lead the construction of all industries. They recognized that there was a

7 Hong Sung Ju, "The Formation of a Science and Technology Policy in South Korea and Its Administrative System: 1945-1967," PhD dissertation, Seoul National University, (Seoul, 2010): 17.

shortage of scientists and technicians in Korea and saw the cultivation of such specialists as an urgent task for the liberated nation. One such argument, as shown by the proposal by An Dong-Hyeok, is a representative case which scientists conceived at that time.

An's proposal for vocational education is reflective of Japan's policy for mobilization of human resources. For An, education in science and technology meant practical and vocational training for a broad range of people, from low-level technicians to experts.[8] During the total war period (1941-1945), the Japanese Government General had decided to reduce the number of liberal arts schools in order to expand vocational schools so that Japanese militarist could mobilize students for work at factories and workspaces for war. The decree for this policy was issued in October 1943. The Japanese government often used such slogans as "Integration of production and education" and "Bring vocation to class" .

Kim Bong-Jip and Lee Tae-Gyu believed that the development of science and technology was needed to ensure the supply commodities. Both scholars insisted on the importance of a unified administration for the development of science and technology. But while Kim benchmarked the Soviets' developmental experience, Lee had in mind the Japanese Empire's science and technology policy, in particular the Japanese Academy of Continental Science in Manchuria. The academy was the central organization for science and technology, simultaneously serving as a research institute and an administrative institution. In a similar vein, Lee called for establishing the Ministry of Science and Technology and argued that all science and industry research institutes should be governed

8 Ibid., 21.

within its jurisdiction.

The ideas of Professor Choe Seong-Se (Engineering College of Kyeongseong University) closely resembled those of Kim. Choe emphasized that the construction of industry in Joseon should be planned and insisted that a socialist planned economy model be implemented in the construction of the new state. He published his ideas mainly in the journals "*Gwahakjeonson* [Front Line of Science]" and "*Inmingwahak* [People's Science]."

In spite of the difference in perspective, both ideas had one thing in common: they agreed that the development of specialists in science and technology had to be fostered in a planned manner. And both opposed the plan for establishing a national university in spite of different political viewpoint. It was common for the students and faculty members of natural science and engineering departments in all universities to believe that the establishment of a national university would downsize education in science and technology by merging a large number of existing national and public higher educational institutions. By setting out to merge educational institutions, the national university plan came to be seen as a move against the promotion of education necessary for increasing the high qualified specialists in science and technology.

However, the policy of the USAMGIK posed an obstacle for the development of science and technology in Korea. U.S. policymakers envisioned the future of Korea as a nation independent from Japan with a viable economy, but the implementation of concrete policies was difficult in light of USAMGIK's limited financial resources.[9] Moreover,

9 "The achievement of this objective will require the progressive elimination of all vestiges

some staff members of the USAMGIK believed that Korea was hardly capable of developing advanced science and technology. Instead, they believed that strengthening Korea's industrial production through the mobilization of labor would be a better solution.[10] In fact, such policies of the USAMGIK were intentionally designed in contrast with Korean communist's policy in the northern area of Korea under the soviet at that time encouraging the development of scientists and technicians, and resulted in a large-scale defection of South Korean scientists and technicians to the North.[11]

In June 1947, the U.S. Educational and Informational Survey Mission was dispatched to Korea for the purpose of supporting the formulation of general and professional education policies. James R. D. Eddy and Douglas N. Batson, who were in charge of investigating vocational education, recommended training teachers under the guidance of visiting American specialists. Eddy and Batson also stated that there was a need to establish a separate division within the Department of Education that would oversee the area of vocational education.

Consequently, disappointed at the policy focusing on vocational

of Japanese control over Korean economic and political life and the eventual substitution of independent Korean governmental, economic and social institutions." Basic Initial Directive to the Commander in Chief, US Army Forces, Pacific, for the Administration of Civil Affairs in Those Areas of Korea Occupied by U.S. Forces, SWNCC 176/8, undated, *Foreign Relations of the United States 1945,* Vol. VI, 1071-1091. There were other policy papers on the financial policy in South Korea. However, there was no mention about US assistance to USAMGIK for that purpose.

10 This idea is very similar to that of Robert Komer, a staff member at NSC in the early 1960s and a friend of Rostow. He recommended to the Park government that labor-intensive light industries would be much better for Korea's industrialization strategy. (Memorandum to Rostow, March 15, 1961, National Security Files (NSF), box 127, John F. Kennedy Library).

11 H. L. "Education," recited from Hong, 34.

training rather than science and technology education, a large number of professors at Seoul National University went to North Korea, Lee Tae-Gyu left for the U.S. in 1949, and Choe Gyu-Nam, who was appointed chief of Bureau of Science and Education in early 1948 under USAMGIK, became a new leader representing scholars in science and technology.[12] He served as the dean of academic affairs at Seoul National University during the USAMGIK period, chief of the Bureau of Science and Education after the establishment of the Korean Government, president of Seoul National University, and the first president of the Korean Physics Society. After obtaining a doctoral degree in Physics from the University of Michigan, Choe returned to Korea and joined the faculty of the Department of Mathematics and Physics in Yeonhi College during the colonial period. In the mid-1950s he served as the Minister of Education, and in the mid-1960s he was a board member of the Economic-Science Review Council.[13]

Officials of the Ministry of Culture and Education under the USAMGIK appointed Raymond W. Phipps as an advisor in vocational training. After three months of investigation, Phipps recommended the establishment of the Bureau of Vocational and Technological Education, which would supervise five sub-divisions: Agricultural Education, Industrial-technical Education, Business and Marketing Education, Girls' and Women's Occupation, and Advancement of Technological Science. The

12 Kim Dong-Kwang, "Haebang Gonggangwa Gwahakja Sahoeui Inyeomjeok Mosaek" ["A Study of the Korean Scientific Community's Grouping for Scientific Ideology in the Period of Liberation, 1945-1953,"] in *Journal of Science and Technology Studies*, 6-1 (2006): 98-118.

13 Choe, Gyu Nam, *Chamjisikgwa Geojitjisik [True Knowledge and Untrue Knowledge]*, (Seoul, 1997).

USAMGIK followed Phipps' recommendation but shortly thereafter had turn over its administrative functions and property to the new government of the Republic of Korea in 1948.

Due to the foregoing limitations in USAMGIK policy, the Republic of Korea government could not attract sufficient capital, posing an impediment to the development of science and technology. With respect to power plants, until the early 1960s the U.S. introduced to Korea only small size thermal power generators, which could meet the short-term demand but could not solve the energy problem in a long-term. This demonstrates that the nature of the U.S. policies toward Korea was not based on a long-term plan but rather on a myopic vision without any particular project in scope.[14]

The Minnesota Plan

After the establishment of the Korean Government, the Ministry of Culture and Education concentrated its efforts in developing and expanding institutions of vocational training. Such policies were justified by the government's stated purpose of increasing the productive population. However, due to the incessant industrial stagnation of the 1950s, they came under the severe criticism by the end of the decade as being unreflective of changes in social and industrial conditions.

14 Park, Tae Gyun, "Continuity or Discontinuity?: The ROK Government's Policy to Recover the Electrical System," Presentation at the AAS annual meeting, (Honolulu, 2011).

The Korean government set up the Bureau of Science Education under the Ministry of Culture and Education, appointing Choe Gyu-Nam as its chief in late 1948. The bureau eliminated the Department of Girls' and Women's Vocation and added the Department of Fisheries Education. Enacted in late 1949, the Education Law stated that "education in citizenship, science, vocation and teacher training deserve special attention."[15]

Soon afterwards, the government announced a policy that sought to adjust the ratio of students in vocational school to students studying the humanities to 6 to 4 in secondary education, and 7 to 3 in higher education.[16] This policy remained in effect after the appointment of Choe as president of Seoul National University. In fact, his appointment to the position demonstrates the prioritization of science and technology by the Korean government.

In 1950, the Ministry of Culture and Education restructured a 6-year secondary education into 3 years of junior high and 3 years of high school. The 248 secondary education institutions that existed at the time of liberation — 183 academic and 65 vocational schools — were reformed into 256 academic high schools and 213 vocational high schools in 1954.

In higher education, four national universities opened colleges of agriculture and engineering, and medical schools and business schools were established in three universities. In addition, several universities expanded existing departments of agriculture and of engineering to the size of colleges, as in the case of Korea University and Dongguk University

15 *Donga Ilbo*, 27 November 1949.

16 *Chosun Daily*, 28 October 1948.

which each established College of Agriculture and College of Forestry in 1951. Chosun University opened its College of Engineering in 1952. As a result of these changes, by December 1954, the number of vocational students (approximately 16,000) in national and public colleges surpassed that of students in the humanities (approximately 13,000).

A plan aimed at strengthening vocational education can also be seen in the character of aid by the United Nations Korean Reconstruction Agency (UNKRA). UNKRA clearly stated that the aid was intended for promoting technical education. Sixty percent of its funds were used for recovery from the devastation of the Korean War and the rest was spent on purchasing equipment for vocational institutes and supporting vocational education.

However, a change in the US policy toward Korea could be seen in the mid 1950s and the Minnesota Plan was a representative case. The plan was devised by the US Foreign Operation Administration (FOA) to support the reconstruction of Seoul National University (SNU) through a partnership with the University of Minnesota, primarily targeting the College of Engineering, College of Agriculture and Forestry, Medical School, and Natural Science. From 1954 to 1962, 9.5 million dollars were invested in the plan, and 218 professors of natural sciences and engineering went to the U.S. for training. This amount accounted for 78% of all aid that the U.S. allocated to Korea's higher education during this period.[17]

17 Kim, Myung-Jin, "A Study on Cooperation in the Field of Higher Education in the 1950s: The Case of SNU-UMN Project," PhD dissertation, Seoul National University, Seoul, 2009.

An important characteristic of the Minnesota Plan is that it did intend to concentrate on the development of science and technology. In contrast to the International Christian University in Japan and Free Berlin University in Western Germany, which were established for the dissemination of American educational philosophy and pedagogical methods to the respected countries, the Minnesota Plan focused on providing aid for science and technology to existing colleges.

Secondly, the primary focus of the project was on providing faculty training. In a broader sense, it was designed to not only help reconstruct SNU but to cultivate scholars and technical specialists who would lead the reconstruction of the nation. Two hundred and eighteen faculty members of SNU were dispatched to the U.S. between January 1, 1955 and June 30, 1962: 57 specialists in agriculture, 64 in engineering, and 78 in medicine (the remaining 27 were recruited from the Department of Public Administration, including 8 public government officials).[18] With respect to the positions of the dispatched personnel at SNU, 54 people were senior faculty members (professors and associate professors), 62 full-time assistant professors and lecturers, 73 teaching assistants, and 20 part-time lecturers (the remaining 16 people were not academic staff, consisting of 8 employees of the College of Nursing and the university hospital and 8 public officers).

Most of the participants in this training program attended or audited courses. Eighty six of them received an academic degree, including 15 obtaining a doctorate. Seventy-one of the program participants received master's degrees: 23 from the College of Agriculture, 4 from the College of Veterinary Science, 21 from the College of Engineering, 11 from

18 Ibid., 58.

medical school, and 12 from the Graduate School of Public Administration.

In terms of distribution of the participants by department, 8 faculty members were dispatched by the department of chemical engineering; 7 each by the departments of electric engineering and mechanical engineering; 6 each by the departments of civil engineering and textile engineering; and 5 each by the departments of aeronautics and marine engineering, optical engineering, and metal engineering. According to a survey conducted in June 1961 among the recipients of the Minnesota Plan training, 11 professors, 16 associate professors, 16 assistant professors, 9 full-time lecturers, and 5 assistants remained at SNU by that time, and one official was still holding office in the university. Those who left SNU obtained tenure positions at other schools such as Hanyang University and KIST, thus continuing their academic career.

Upon returning from training in the University of Minnesota, numerous professors of science and technology attempted to introduce new courses and teaching methods. Their endeavors often led to conflict with faculty members who were educated during the colonial period, or after liberation without the opportunity to study abroad. On the other hand, students had great expectations for the Minnesota-trained professors.[19]

Overall, since the establishment of SNU in 1946, approximately 86% of full-time professors at the College of Engineering gained an opportunity to travel abroad for study or as a field trip. Seventy-five per cent of them went to the U.S. with the assistance of the US International Cooperation Administration [ICA], which had succeeded the FOA in

19 Ibid., 85-89.

1955.

Along with faculty training, the Minnesota Plan also supplied new equipment to educational facilities at Seoul National University playing an important role in the overall Americanization of the structure and culture within the College of Engineering. In the period between 1955 and 1959, a total of 2.7 million U.S. dollars were spent on the provision of equipment. The largest portion-1.38 million U.S. dollars-was allocated for the College of Engineering, whereas 0.34 and 0.74 million dollars, respectively, were used for the College of Agriculture and medical school.

The Americanization of teaching and research methods at the College of Engineering was further facilitated by the American professors who were dispatched by the University of Minnesota to serve as advisors. Particularly prominent among them was Clarence Weems, an MIT graduate who spoke fluent Korean.[20] Most of the American professors focused more on the practical connections between school and industry rather than on theoretical knowledge, and valued experimenting and other forms of practice over lectures.

In sum, the Minnesota Plan made a major contribution to converting education at the College of Engineering into a more American system. As a result of the plan, the number of students continuing their research in the U.S. rapidly increased.

The Minnesota Plan was supported by the U.S. government within the framework of American technological aid to Korea. The plan for

20 Clarence Weems seems to be a son of a missionary, William Weems, who had served in Korea during the colonial period. He was as fluent in the Korean language as a native speaker.

technological aid to Korea became concrete during the second half of the Eisenhower administration, with the formulation of policies towards Korea in the National Security Council Report of 1957.[21] The chronology of events illustrates that the Minnesota Plan started prior to materialized technological aid, and points to a close connection between the Plan and U.S. aid for the reconstruction and economic development of Korea.

However, the Eisenhower Administration generally did not prioritize providing economic and technical aid to developing countries, including Korea.[22] The provision of aid was stipulated by the Military Security Act which focused more on security rather than economic and technical assistance, and reducing the size of foreign aid was a key objective of the administration's New Look policy. [23] Therefore, the U.S. aid for the development of science and technology in Korea cannot be considered as a plan with a long-term vision. In fact, the Minnesota Plan was originally envisioned as a three- or four-year program, but only later extended until 1962.

In addition, there were a number of negative responses to the effect of technological aid under the Minnesota Plan. The criticism targeted not only the Minnesota Plan, but also the work of the Oregon Advisory Group, a group dispatched to Korea to support its economic development plan. Most of the complains were derived from communication

---

21 *National Security Council Report*, NSC 5702, 14 January 1957, FRUS 1955-1957 Vol. XXIII, part 2, 374-384.

22 Diane B. Kunz, "Cold War Dollar Diplomacy: The Other Side of Containment," in *The Diplomacy of the Crucial Decade: American Foreign Relations During the 1960s*, eds., Diane B. Kunz (New York, 1994).

23 Park, Tae Gyun, "Changes in US Policy Toward South Korea in the Early 1960s," *Korean Studies*, 23, (1999).

issues and the unilateral decision-making by American advisors, as there existed few reciprocal processes between the American and Korean scholars and administrators involved.

Nevertheless, the Minnesota Plan is critical to understanding the history of of Korean science and technology. In spite of the conflicts that arose from the methodological changes, the Minnesota Plan initiated reliance of Korean science and technology on the American academia of science and technology. It should be noted that there were no other alternatives to the U.S.-oriented transformation, given the ultimate importance of the U.S. for the national security of South Korea in the years following the Korean War. It was inevitable one under the Cold War system in a frontline. .

The Vietnam War, the Establishment of KIST, and the Heavy Chemical Industrialization Policy

No development policy for science and technology was actually implemented during the 1950s at the national level except established in Korea was the Institute of Atomic Energy Research.[24] Rather, the starting point of such a policy can be traced to the First Five-Year Plan for Promotion of Technology of 1962.[25] There was also a plan to found an

24 Koh, Dae Seung, "The Process and Background of Establishing Korean Atomic Institute," MA dissertation, Seoul National University, Seoul, 1991.

25 Moon, Manyong, "1960Nyeondae Gwahakgisul Bum: Hangugui Hyeondaejeok Gwahakgisulchejeui Hyeongseong" ["The Science and Technology Boom in 1960s: The Formation of Science and Technology System in Korea,"], *Journal of the Korean History of Science Society*, 29-1 (2007).

institute, tentatively named Korea Institute of Science and Technology, in early 1962, as well as a proposal to establish an integrated science and technology research center under the Ministry of Commerce and Industry in 1963, but neither was implemented due to fundraising difficulties. In fact, the U.S. at that time was focused on the development of labor-intensive light industries in Korea and discounted the idea of building high technology or heavy chemical industries. Such a stance sheds the light on the difficulty of allocating resources for building steel mills and machinery factories under the First Five-Year Economic Development Plan.[26]

Rather, during the military government and beginning of civilian government under Park Chung Hee, scientific and technological policies was scaled back as the Bureau of Science and Technology was downsized within the Ministry of Culture and Education, and the activities of the Institute of Atomic Energy Research had to be decreased. The prioritization of simple industrial training over science led to a further decline in the promotion of basic sciences.[27]

The promotion of science and technology finally kicked into gear in the mid-1960s when Korea sent combat units to the Vietnam War. During the Johnson-Park summit in 1965, it was announced that the U.S. would provide Korea with 150 million dollars as a developmental loan and would consider supporting a research center for applied sciences. To

---

26 Song, Sungsoo, "Hanguk Jonghapjecheolsaeopgyehoegui Byeoncheongwajeong, 1958~1969" ["The Historical Development of Integrated Steelworks Plans in Korea, 1958~1969,"], *Journal of the Korean History of Science Society*, 24-1 (2002): 7-9.

27 Kim, Geun Bae, "A Study on the Process of Establishing KIST," MA dissertation, Seoul National University, Seoul, 1989, 240-243.

this end, President Johnson also offered to dispatch scientific advisors to assist the development of industrial technology and the establishment of the research center.

Such a shift was enabled by the popularity of Walt Whitman Rostow's view that foreign aid was crucial for the modernization of developing countries and emerging nations, and also by the Johnson Administration's attention to technological aid.[28] Yet the primary recipients of this technological aid consisted of major U.S. allies in the Cold War, such as Japan, Israel and the European nations, while less economically developed countries, such as Korea, were hardly seen as targets of such policies. Korea, therefore, could not count on the U.S. technological grants until the Vietnam War, which became the turning point in the U.S. provision of technological aid to Korea.

In addition, the Rostow's rise within the Johnson Administration allowed the American government to change its policy toward Korea. Rostow had not occupied a decisive position during the Kennedy Administration in spite of the fact that his view of foreign assistance was widespread within the government. After the assassination of President Kennedy, Rostow was appointed as Special Assistant for National Security Affairs Furthermore, since he was a strong proponent of increased involvement in Vietnam and mobilization of allied forces, increased aid became feasible for countries that sent troops to Vietnam. South Korea, in particular, sent the second largest group of combat troops during the Vietnam War.

---

28 Park, Tae Gyun, *Ubanggwa Jegug, Hanmigwangye-ui Du Sinhwa[An Ally and Empire: Two Myths in the Korea-U.S. Relationship]*, (Seoul, 2012).

The U.S. focused its provisions of technological aid to applied research centers rather than to universities and other educational institutions. The Korean government requested additional American aid for the establishment of research institutes and was prepared to allocate more resources from its own budget, but the U.S. maintained that funding had to be based on industrial demands from the private sector. American policymakers at the time believed that scientists should deliver faster results as remuneration of private-sector investment, which was very different from ideas of Korean officials and scientists who stressed government's leading role in stimulating developing science and technology. They also expected that students who were pursuing degrees in the U.S. at the time would return to their homeland and contribute to the development of Korea's science and technology.

Following President Johnson's proposal, the two governments carried forward the plan for a science and technology research center. The plan materialized into the "Agreement on the U.S.-Korea Collaboration in Establishing and Operating the Korea Institute of Science and Technology (KIST)," signed by both parties on February 4, 1966. The agreement stated that the "affiliated research institute will support the organization and operation of this Institute, train researchers and administrators to enhance its capacity, and strive to open the door and contribute to international exchange of technology," making it clear that the institute had to be open to international exchange and linked to the U.S. In other words, connections to industry and to the U.S. were preconditions for the establishment of KIST.

In accordance with the U.S. plan for the research institute in Korea, the Battelle Memorial Institute (Battelle) played an important role in the process of establishing KIST. Battelle's support took place in two stages: the first occurred from 1966 to 1967, and the second continued until June 1971. In the first stage, it not only provided overall advice but was also directly involved in devising the specific contents of KIST's activities–e.g., helping find and select scientists and technicians, cooperating and advising on technological development, conducting applied research, supporting the installation of information channels for science, technology and industrial economy. Through this process, it was decided by Korean government and scientists that the priorities for KIST would be material engineering, mechanical engineering, electrical engineering, chemistry, and food engineering.[29]

As the majority of scholars point out, the establishment of KIST was the critical turning point in the development of Korea's science and technology. Each step in the process of the institute's foundation - the U.S. support, links with the U.S., recruitment of U.S.-educated researchers - determined the future direction of Korea's scientific and technological development. Although the U.S. aid allowed Korea to achieve a rapid growth in the way of technology, specified priorities for the received aid resulted in an imbalanced underdevelopment of basic sciences.

Along with the establishment of KIST, the Vietnam War also led the Park government to develop the idea for its own military industry. Even though the Johnson Administration was reluctant to allow South Korea to build its own military industry, President Park and his staff relentlessly persisted in discussing the possibility with the American government. The idea in fact originated from the Brown Memorandum of

29 Kim, "A Study on the Process of Establishing KIST,".

1966, which promised the "modernization of firepower communication, and maneuverability of the Korean Army."[30] There was not much progress during the war, however, until the Nixon Doctrine and the following withdrawal of a division of the U.S.F.K. with the accompanying pledge that the U.S. would "modernize the equipment of the Korean Army and provide long-term military aid."[31]

Since 1948, the U.S. had adhered to a policy of restricting the development of Korea's defense industry. There were two reasons for this policy. First, there was a risk that such a development would provoke North Korea, specifically given that President Rhee Syngman's insisting of unification by "marching North" and his objections to signing the armistice agreement was a source conflict between the two Koreas. The development of a military industry in South Korea would create a security dilemma for the Korean Peninsula. As a result, beginning with the NSC 8 pf 1949 and until the late 1960s, the U.S. policy towards South Korea was to restrict the increase of Korea's military power and to scale down its military industry. Furthermore, the US government was particularly concerned about the security crises of 1967 and 1968, partially triggered by the Park government's active retaliation strategy. [32]

The second reason was that developing Korea's defense indus-

30 The Brown Memorandum was joined between the Johnson Administration and the ROK government in March 1966 which defined the special assistance to Korea at the expense of sending Korean combat troop to Vietnam. It covered the more than three hundred million dollar economic and technical assistance as well as military aid. Brown was name of American Ambassador in Seoul at the time.

31 O Won-Chul, *The Korea Story: President Park Jung-hee's leadership and the Korean industrial revolution*, (Seoul, 2009).

32 Park, Tae Gyun, "Beyond the Myth: Reassessing the Security Crisis on the Korean Peninsula in the Mid 1960s," *Pacific Affairs* 82-1 (2009).

try could aggravate the security situation in the region at large. Since South Korea was competing not only with North Korea, China, and the U.S.S.R., but also with Japan, the development of Korea's defense industry could lead to an accelerated arms race among the neighboring countries. The consideration of such a possibility was clearly reflected in the U.S. efforts to prevent South Korea from developing a nuclear bomb and missiles and from enhancing the capacity of its navy and air force.

Nevertheless the Vietnam War paved the way for the South Korean government's vision of building a new country with its own military capacity. In addition to South Korea, other countries involved in the Vietnam War, such as Thailand and the Philippines, simultaneously started to develop their own military industries in the late 1960s and early 1970s. In this respect, the Vietnam War brought about significant changes to the region. Since South Korea participated in the war at the request of the U.S., the American government could not easily reject its demands. In the words of William J. Porter, the U.S. ambassador to Korea at that time, the dispatch of Korean troops to Vietnam was like an "Aladdin's Lamp" for the Korean government.[33]

The Nixon Doctrine: Another Turning Point

Ironically, an important factor that facilitated the transfer of mili-

33 "Additional ROK Troop Contribution to Vietnam," Telegram From the Embassy in Korea to the Department of State, Seoul, 25 November 1967, 0528Z, *FRUS 1964~1968*. Vol. XXIX

tary technology was the Nixon Doctrine, which weakened America's engagement in Asia by stressing the "Asianization" of regional defense issues. Even though the Johnson Administration allowed special aid to Korea due to its contribution to the Vietnam War, the administration had been reluctant to promote military industry in South Korea.

But the Nixon Doctrine, which caused a reduction of U.S. forces in South Korea, inevitably brought change of President Park's policies. President Park strongly protested the downsizing of U.S. forces in South Korea and requested a transfer of military technology that had been prohibited until the late 1960s. The Nixon Administration allowed the building of a military industry in limited ways beginning in 1970, not only for the sake of maintaining a balance of power on the Korean Peninsula after the withdrawal of American forces, but also to appease Park's anger. In July 1970, President Park began to consider the possibility of manufacturing the M16 gun and several kinds of small canons.[34]

Using the opportunity provided under the Nixon Doctrine, the Park Administration was able to set up research facilities for national defense in the 1970s. The Agency for Defense Development (ADD) was established in August 1970 (it later became a private corporation). The location of the ADD, which was situated adjacent to KIST, hints at the link between Korean science and technology, and national defense.[35] ADD along with KIST became the leading center of the development of Kore-

34 A lot of Documents documents produced in the Blue House in 1969 and 1970 showing the Park government's intention to build military industry are now declassified in the ROK Presidential Library. They show heated debates between the Nixon and the Park administrations regarding the military industry.

35 Moon, "1960Nyeondae Gwahakgisul Bum", 80.

an science and technology in the mid-1970s and was commonly referred as the "place where all great brains in science gathered."

Another transition resulted from the change in the role played by Japan in Northeast Asia. According to Rostow's plan, Japan, instead of the U.S., would broaden its role in Asia. In order to expand economic aid to developing countries, the participation of other developed countries such as Japan and those in Western Europe would be needed.[36] Normalization between Korea and Japan was one of the significant objectives for both the Kennedy and the Johnson Administrations because the U.S. sought to transfer a heavy portion of the burden of the Korean Peninsula onto Japan. This purpose was strengthened during the Nixon Administration due to the economic problems caused by the Vietnam War. Although the transfer was delayed due to the prominence of Korean combat troops at the frontline in Vietnam, shortly after inauguration of President Nixon, the U.S. began to encourage Japan to play a greater in Northeast Asia. The U.S. intention became apparent during the summit between Nixon and the Japanese Prime Minister Sato in late 1969.

From the perspective of the Korean government, the normalization of relations with Japan in 1965 stood for another chance to revive its original plans. It is a well-known fact that the funds obtained through claims from Japan during the normalization talks greatly contributed to Korea's economic development. In particular, the Pohang Steel Mill project benefited greatly from the normalization. Since the beginning of the administration and until the late 1960s, steel mill construction had been

36 Walt W. Rostow, and Max Milikan, *A Proposal: Key to an Effective Foreign Policy*. (New york, 1957): 84

one of President Park's main ambitions, but the realization of the project had continued to be delayed due to the shortage of funds and necessary technology.[37]

Park considered the steel industry to be a key to building an industrial nation and to serve as a foundation for heavy and military industries. He once said to Kim Jeong-Ryeom, Minister of Commerce, that "the power of Japan to initiate the Pacific war came from steel mills. They had steel mills, and thus made tanks, cannons, and warships." For Park, Japan–and specifically, its Kawasaki Steel Mill–was a model for his vision of Korea.

At the end of 1966, soon after Kim Hak-Ryul was appointed vice premier, the Research Committee of Overall Planning for Steel Business was organized with the participation of KIST scholars, like Kim Jae-Gwan and Yun Yeo-Gyeong. But a more important task was acquiring financial and technological assistance from Japan. In September 1965, the Japanese Ministry of Industry, in cooperation with Japan Steel Federation and the six largest steel companies in Japan, dispatched to Korea a group of 9 specialists. Japan provided approximately 60% of the construction costs and most of the equipment during the first stage of the project (1970-1973). In the construction process, a coalition of Japan steel companies called Japan Group advised their Korean counterparts and advised them in sectors of skills and equipments.

The usage of funds obtained through claims filed through normalization talks was originally restricted to the agricultural sector and was to be spent evenly each year for a period of 10 years. If Korea wanted to

37 Song, 6-12.

use the funds within a short period of time and for a different purpose, it first had to seek Japan's agreement. For this reason, KIST prepared a specific plan for steel mill construction and presented it to the Japanese government. Japan approved the plan at the first Korea-Japan Ministerial Meeting in August 1969. A month later, a 13-member group consisting of Japanese government officials from the Ministries of Economy, Defense, Finance, and Foreign Affairs, and experts from the private companies such as Fuji Steel, was dispatched to Korea to verify the feasibility of the project.

In November 1969, a negotiation team led by Jeong Mun-Do, Assistant Secretary of the Economic Planning Board, visited Japan. Here, a controversy between Korea and Japan arose in relation to the type of casting and rolling facilities to be constructed. The Japanese argued that the facilities proposed by the Korean side were too advanced and not yet available even in Japan. Eventually, Koreans agreed to reduce some of their proposals for the facilities and to change the casting method to be employed.

Negotiations on the terms of financing the project resulted in a pledge by Japan to provide 73.7 million dollars out of the claim funds during the three-year period, and an additional 50 million in the form of a commercial loan. Then, on December 3, 1969, Kim Hak-Ryul, Deputy Prime Minister of Korean Economic Planning Board and Japanese Ambassador to Korea, Masahide Kaneyama, signed the Agreement between Korea and Japan on the Construction of Pohang Iron and Steel Company. From this point, the cooperation proceeded mostly in relation to the technological aspect. In December 1969, Pohang Steel made a preliminary technological contract with Japanese companies Yawata Steel, Fuji

Steel, and Nihon Steel Pipe.

The technological transfers and advice from Japan, as well as its collaboration, appear to have been as important as the funding. In September 1966, the first television set was made in Korea by Kumsung Company. It was an assembly achieved by a technological cooperation with the Japanese company Hitachi, with 75% of components imported from Japan. Since then, Korean exports in electronics as a percentage of total exports surged from 1% in 1965 to 6.7% in 1969.

A visit by Doko Toshio, the president of Toshiba, to the Blue House in 1966 appers to have played an important role as well.(O 2009, 312) Doko pointed out that the world was entering an age of electronics industry and advised Korea to build factories for electronics and electronic components.

The Korea Electronic Industries Cooperative (KEIC) was formed on January 12, 1967 and on May 30, 1967, released a draft bill entitled the Promotion of Electronics Industry Bill. The bill was a rehashing of a Japanese legislation of the same title that was enacted on May 11, 1957. (Nishino 2004, 141) In October 1967, KEIC dispatched an observation team to Japan and in July 1970, established an office in Tokyo. The Korean city of Gumi was designated as an electronics industrial complex, and in September 1969, a Japanese businessman of Korean origin, Gwak Tae-Seok, founded Toshiba Korea in Gumi.

Koreans also borrowed the Japanese model of industrial restructuring, which had allowed Japanese heavy chemical industry to achieve a 10-billion U.S. dollar mark in exports within 10 years after the beginning of production in 1957. The government's plan for restructuring Korean industries, presented in late 1972, was based on the strong belief that

Korea needed to adopt a similar model. On January 12, 1973, President Park announced the beginning of heavy chemical industrialization at the annual New Year's press conference.

The plan for heavy chemical industrialization envisioned an intensive fostering of the machine industry during the period of 1973-1981, and particularly emphasized the growth of the defense industry. The role model for the mechanization of the defense industry was the Japanese company Hitachi.[38] A machine manufacturer, Hitachi produced all kinds of mechanical products, from large-size engines to be used in power plants and warships, to trains and weapons.[39] At a routine ministerial meeting between Korea and Japan, the Korean government requested assistance from the Japanese government and proposed an organization of non-governmental economic exchanges for the process of heavy chemical industrialization.[40]

Conclusion

This chapter examined the reorientation of South Korean science and technology from a system linked predominantly to Japan during the

38 O Won-Chul, *The Korea Story: President Park Jung-hee's leadership and the Korean industrial revolution*, (Seoul, 2009), 570.

39 The South Korean government sent mission teams to Japan several times to benchmark weapons technology, according to classified documents found in the Presidential Library of Korea. Another document shows that the South Korean government invited Japanese technicians to stay for longer than a year in South Korea.

40 Nishino Junya, "Learning from Japan and Transformation of South Korean Industrial Policy: Focusing on the 1960-1970s," PhD dissertation, Yonsei University, Seoul, 2004, 212-220.

colonial period to one dominated by U.S. standards and priorities after liberation. U.S. policies during the Cold War era became a major determinant of the scientific and technological development of Korea, bringing about key aspects such as stagnant science and technology policies following the country's liberation, the Minnesota Plan of the 1950s, the establishment of KIST in 1966, transfers of advanced technology from Japan in the 1960s and 1970s, the correlation between the dispatch of the Korean troops to Vietnam and the development of the defense and heavy chemical industries in the 1970s. Such policies led to rapid scientific and technological progress, but at the same time limited the scale and direction of the development.

It is undoubtedly true that U.S. policies initiated the development of Korea's science and technology in the late 1960s, but we should also be aware that U.S. policies had hindered such a development in an earlier period. In short, U.S. policies and the circumstances of the Cold War did not always promote growth within Korea.

This point is easily be demonstrated by examining the contents of the agreements and pacts reached between Korea and the U.S. regarding technology and science. Both the 1956 Agreement for Cooperation Concerning Civil Use of Atomic Energy and the 1961 Comprehensive Agreement Regarding Economic Technical Assistance between the Government of Republic of Korea and the Government of the United States entail the provision of technical and scientific assistance by the U.S., while simultaneously stipulating American control over the technological development.

This article does not intend to understate the contribution of the Korean government officials, scientists, and technicians of the era. Regardless of the amount of American aid, the development of science and technology in Korea would ultimately have been impossible without the enthusiastic efforts of these domestic actors. In fact, considering the restraints imposed on Korea by the U.S., as mentioned in the above discussion of KIST, the role of Korean actors in Korea's development cannot be underestimated. This thesis does not refute the model of scientific and technological development under the theory of the developmental state. Rather, it aims to clarify the facts that, given the circumstances of the Cold War and Korea's strategic location, its science and technology could not avoid the effect of geopolitics and the U.S. Cold War strategy, in both positive and negative ways.

A limitation of this study is that it did not deeply examine the issues related to the theories and substantive elements of science and technology. A closer scrutiny of the process of choosing a particular direction of development among several options would strengthen the argument of this thesis. To this end, a specialized understanding of science and technology in the U.S. and Japan, as well as in the communist and Western European countries, is needed. This task requires an integrated effort of specialists in the humanities and social science in addition to those in science and technology. A potential area of future research includes comparative approaches examining the differences and similarities between the case of Korea and that of other countries.

The Historical Development of Technological Capabilities in Korean Steel Industry

The Case of POSCO*

Sungsoo Song

Introduction

Korean capitalism continued to develop through the compressed industrialization from the 1960s to the 1990s. Studies on the industrialization of Korea have focused on the role of the government, large corporations, and labor, gradually concerning themes such as technological development. Studies on technological development have emphasized the concept of technological capabilities, and are summed up by Park Woohee and Bae Yongho's *Hangugui Gisulbaljeon [Korea's Technological Development]*, Kim Linsu's *Imitation to Innovation* (1997), and Lee Keun, et al.'s *Hanguksaneobui Gisulleungnyeokgwa Gyeongjaengnyeok [Technological Capabilities and Competitiveness of Korean Industries]*.[1] Based on these

* This paper is based on Sungsoo Song, "Tegisulleungnyeok Baljeonui Sigibyeol Teukseong: Pohangjecheol Saryeyeongute" ["Historical Perspectives on the Development of

achievements, recent studies have attempted to redefine the stages and types of development of technological capabilities in Korea. For instance, Kim Linsu recomposed technological development stages into duplicative imitation, creative imitation, and innovation, and Lee Keun and Lim Chaisung categorized the types of technological catch-up into path-following catch-up, stage-skipping catch-up and path-creating catch-up.[2]

These research achievements have contributed greatly to understanding the development of technological capabilities in Korea, but are deemed to have the following problems. First, existing studies on the development of technological capabilities generally focus on the logical completion of theories, but do not pay sufficient attention to exploring historical facts. Second, previous studies have analyzed the development of technological capabilities of many industries, but major industries that contributed to Korean industrialization including the iron and steel industry have not been sufficiently explored, and even where research has been carried out, the study does not span the entire timeframe of the industry. Third, most of the existing studies are only able to briefly describe the process of technological development, and analyze its success factors,

---

Technological Capabilities: A Case Study on POSCO"], *Journal of Technology Innovation* 10-1 (2002), 174-200, I partially revised and updated the previous paper.

1 Park Woohee and Bae Yongho, *Hangugui Gisulbaljeon [Korea's Technological Development]* (Seoul, 1996); Kim Linsu, *Imitation to Innovation: The Dynamics of Korea's Technological Learning* (Boston, 1997); Lee Keun, et al., *Hanguksaneobui Gisulleungnyeokgwa Gyeongjaengnyeok [Technological Capabilities and Competitiveness of Korean Industries]* (Seoul, 1997)

2 Kim Linsu, "Building Technological Capability for Industrialization: Analytical Frameworks and Korea's Experience," *Industrial and Corporate Change* 8-1 (1999), 111-136; Lee Keun and Lim Chaisung, "Technological Regimes, Catching-up and Leapfrogging: Findings from the Korean Industries," *Research Policy* 30- 3 (2001), 459-483.

therefore, with a few exceptions aside, what momentum technological capabilities were developed and what features technological activities had during each period are still left in the black box.

Based on the awareness of such problems, this paper seeks to examine the historical development process of technological capabilities in the iron and steel industry in Korea through the case of Pohang Iron and Steel Company (포항제철). Established as a public enterprise in 1968, Pohang Iron and Steel Company grew by leaps and bounds, with the construction of the Pohang Steelworks (포항제철소) in the 1970s and Gwangyang Steelworks (광양제철소) in the 1980s. The company was completely privatized in 2000 and renamed as POSCO in 2002. In terms of output, POSCO was the world's third largest steelmaker from 1990 to 1992, and the second from 1993 to 1997. In 1998, 1999, and 2001, the company made the very top of the list. Since 2002, POSCO has fallen back in the rankings as the world's 4th or 5th largest steelmaker as a result of merges between large steel producers in Europe and Japan.

Technological development of POSCO has been studied by Byun

Unit: 1,000 tons, %

Year	1970	1975	1980	1985	1990	1995	2000	2005
Production capacity (POSCO)	504 (-)	2,534 (1,234)	8,558 (5,903)	13,539 (9,284)	23,125 (16,223)	36,772 (23,428)	43,107 (27,735)	47,812 (31,420)
Share of global steel industry	0.1	0.4	1.2	1.9	3.0	4.9	5.1	4.2
Share of GDP	0.4	1.1	1.5	1.9	1.9	2.0	1.7	2.5

Table 1. Development of the Korean Steel Industry (From 1970 to 2005) [Source: Bank of Korea Iron and Steel Association]

Hyungyun, Park Woohee, Alice H. Amsden, Anthony P. D'Costa, and Sung Jowhan.[3] Studies by Byun, Park, and Amsden examined several features evinced in the course of POSCO's technological development, but are limited to the 1970s. Using the notions of "structural competitiveness" and "reverse exploitation strategy" respectively, D'Costa and Sung analyzed technological achievements of POSCO, but did not give sufficient description on the process of the technological development. In contrast to these studies, this paper seeks to explain and analyze features of POSCO's technological activities considering the entire timeframe from the 1970s to the 1990s, and thus contribute to finding out the whole mechanism in the development of technological capabilities.

To this end, this paper explored historical facts through POSCO's company history, newspapers, memoirs and essays, in addition to existing literature. In particular, I carried out in-depth interviews with major actors who had been deeply involved in technological activities at POSCO. This paper reconstructs the stages of technological development into technological acquisition in the 1970s, technological catch-up in the 1980s, and technological creation since the 1990s. During interviews, I confirmed that the major actors held notions of acquisition, catch-up and creation for each period. Hence, these notions are deemed to be based on

3 Byun Hyungyun, "Hangukcheolganggongeobui Gisulchukjeok: Pohangjecheoleul Jungsimeuro" ["Technological Accumulation in Korea's Steel Industry: A Case Study on POSCO"], *Economic Journal* 19-2 (1980): 124-136; Alice H. Amsden, *Asia's Next Giant: South Korea and Late Industrialization* (New York, 1989), 291-318; Anthony P. D'Costa, "State, Steel and Strength: Structural Competitiveness and Development in South Korea," *Journal of Development Studies* 31-1 (1994): 44-81; Park Woohee and Bae Yongho, *Hangugui Gisulbaljeon,* 161-197; Sung Jowhan, "A Study on the Process of Technological Development in the Korean Steel Industry: POSCO's Reverse Exploitation Strategy", PhD Dissertation, Kookmin Univeristy, Seoul, 1999.

"following the actors", as referred to widely in sociology of science and technology.[4]

Technological Acquisition Started by Overseas Training

In the 1970s, overseas training was main route through which POSCO acquired technologies necessary for constructing and operating steel mills. This is well evinced in POSCO's official record: "The successful construction of factories and normal operations were made possible thanks to the results of overseas training."[5] Technologies that existed in the domestic steel industry at the time were limited to operating small-scale equipment in certain specific processes, so POSCO had to depend on advanced countries in order to acquire technologies necessary for operating large-scale comprehensive steel mills.

POSCO selected overseas training candidates two-fold, and the in-house training, which the candidates had to undergo prior to being sent abroad, included education on some basic knowledge of the steel industry, as well as etiquettes and attitudes to be aware of in a foreign working environment. Final candidates were organized into respective

4 Bruno Latour, *Science in Action: How to Follow Scientists and Engineers through Society* (Cambridge, 1987); Wiebe E. Bijker, "The Social Construction of Fluorescent Lighting, or How an Artifact Was Invented in Its Diffusion," Wiebe E. Bijker and John Law eds., *Shaping Technology / Building Society: Studies in Sociotechnical Change* (Cambridge, 1992), 75-105.

5 POSCO, *Pohangjecheol 7Nyeonsa:Ilgwanjecheolso Geonseolgirok [POSCO in 7 Years: Construction Records of Integrated Steel Mill]* (Pohang, 1975), 526.

teams, assigned specific purposes of overseas training, and were given intensive education on their core tasks.[6] Moreover, before relevant staff left for their respective overseas training institutes, POSCO gave a mindset education which was designed to instill in them the importance of their current jobs for the nation, and even instructed them to thoroughly learn technologies on a man-to-man basis, regardless of official contracts or schedules.[7]

POSCO sent trainees mostly to Japan Group (JG) comprised of Nippon Steel Company (NSC, 新日本鐵鋼) and Nippon Kokan (NKK, 日本鋼管), and Japan at that time was positively cooperative in transferring technologies to POSCO. For instance, Kim Gihong (김기홍), who received training in the Muroran (室蘭) steel mill in 1969, recollected: "Eminent personnel from the Japanese steel industry gave lectures", and "thanks to the characteristics of the Japanese people, such as precision and kindness, I could grasp the various concepts of the steel industry in just three months."[8] Likewise, Hong Sangbok (홍상복), who as supervisor in the steelmaking department received training in NKK in 1972, recollected: "The company, competing with its elder brother-like NSC, was more eager to teach trainees, and provide whatever data trainees requested."[9]

POSCO's trainees actively participated in the overseas training programs with great enthusiasm. They jotted down lectures in detail, in-

6 Ibid., 527-531.

7 Park Taejoon, *Sinjongisangajok [New Kind of Separate Family]* (Pohang, 1987), 238. Park Taejoon was president of POSCO from 1968 to 1993. For the biography of Park Taejoon, see Seo Kapkyung., *The Steel King: The Story of T. J. Park* (New York, 1997).

8 Lee Ho ed., *Sindeullin Saramdeurui Hapchang: Pohangjecheol 30Nyeon Iyagi* [Chorus of Bewitched People: POSCO in 30 Years] (Seoul, 1998), 264-265.

9 My Interview with Hong Sangbok, 23 November 2000.

cessantly asked questions to lecturers, and memorized what they could not understand in belief that it would be of great use someday.[10] Also, the trainees collected and copied whatever was deemed would be helpful for the operation of steel mills. In this regard, one of technological staffs at JG recollected: "they (trainees) appeared to have been ordered by their company to bring as much data as possible, or they applied a formula whereby their training performance was evaluated by the thickness of the data they brought home."[11] Moreover, POSCO trainees complemented their knowledge through personal relations with JG engineers. For instance, Kim Jongjin (김종진), who led the trainees in hot rolling process at the early stage of POSCO, recollected: "our team approached Japanese engineers with all means available including treating them to dinner with drinks … When design drawings were spotted, we were quick in slipping them into pockets or tried to memorize them as much as possible, even though we were quite drunk."[12]

POSCO intended to maximize the benefits of education and training program by systematically managing and utilizing the overseas trainees. Trainees were required to report before and after the overseas training, and trainees dispatched for over two months must make intermediate reports twice a month. Also, trainees were assigned to their professional fields, and worked mandatorily for POSCO for two years after the program. More importantly, POSCO included gathering of training

10 Lee, *Sindeullin Saramdeurui Hapchang* , 159.

11 Toshihiko Ariga, et al., *Memoirs of POSCO's Construction: A Record of Technological Cooperation with Korea* [有賀敏彦 外, 『浦項綜合製鐵の建設回顧錄: 韓國への技術協力の記錄』], (Tokyo, 1997), 154, 168.

12 Lee Ho, *Nuga Saebyeogeul Taeuneunga?: Baktaejun Cheorui Iryeokseo [Who Burns the Dawn?: Park Taejoon's Personal History in Steel]* (Seoul, 1992), 239-240.

data and providing in-house training in the overseas trainees' responsibilities. Nearly all the materials brought back by the trainees were preserved as microfilms, which were used to educate other employees or make POSCO's technology plans. The overseas trainees endeavored to transfer their new knowledge and fresh ideas through in-house training.[13]

Most of the technology obtained by POSCO through overseas training was for plant operations, which was already mature and standardized in the developed countries. Because POSCO's overseas training targeted mature technology, it was relatively easy for the company to acquire the technology and obtain visible results in a short period of time. In the case of the steel industry, however, it was impossible to accumulate operation technology without actually operating the facilities, and production processes were not sufficiently computerized in the early 1970s, so this made on-the-job training even more important. Moreover, considering that Korean iron and steel industry had no experience in the operation of comprehensive steel mills, operation technology for large facilities can be interpreted as a kind of state-of-the-art technology at the time.[14]

While acquiring operation technology through overseas training, POSCO wanted to reach normal capacity as soon as possible through systematic preparation for plant operations. POSCO formed an operations group and a maintenance group from the beginning rather than after the plant construction, putting the former in charge of construction

13 POSCO, *Pohangjecheol 10 Nyeonsa [POSCO in 10 Years]* (Pohang, 1979), 165-166.

14 For more discussion about the characteristics of technological transfer from Japan to POSCO, see Sungsoo Song, "Technological Acquisition in Early POSCO," 329-348, esp. 339-342.

work and assigning the latter to supervise the construction.[15] POSCO also wanted to preempt potential problems due to defects in facilities by test operating the facilities before plant construction was completed. For instance, its iron-making department provided technological staffs with professional training in three stages in February-May, 1973, in preparation for operations.[16] This can explain the technological reason why POSCO was able to make profits, just one year after its plants began operation.

After real operations started, the university-graduate engineers who received overseas training took charge of operations in each process, the other technicians and skilled workers supported these engineers, and Japanese technicians provided advice. POSCO's university-graduate engineers played a supporting role during overseas training, but played a leading role at operation sites. The company hired Japanese on-site technicians who had retired in their mid-50s as technical consultants for one year or two years to allow its workers to gain valuable on-the-job experience.[17]

Although accidents and mishaps were inevitable in the early stages, the employees at POSCO rapidly became accustomed to operating the plant, and POSCO's operation technology improved at a rapid pace. For example, keeping in mind the operational capacity of Japanese steelworks that were of similar sizes as the blast furnace of Pohang Steelworks, JG advised that POSCO's daily production would reach its design capacity

---

15 *POSCO, Pohangjecheol 7Nyeonsa*, 341.

16 Ibid., 608-613.

17 My Interview with Lee Ilok, 30 June 1999.

in 12 months. However, POSCO aimed to reach the normal capacity within six months, and moreover, managed to shorten it to 107 days.[18] After the plant secured normal operations, the company's dependence on foreign technicians sharply decreased, and it acquired sufficient on-site know-how within four or five months of operational experience. The decline in its dependence on foreign technicians was confirmed by the facts that starting with the project for Pohang Works Phase 2, guidance on operations was not included in the technical service contract with JG, and that the contract to hire retired Japanese technicians as technical consultants was terminated.

POSCO could fast acquire operations technologies mainly because of good policies on managing technological manpower. First, university-graduated engineers were assigned as foremen on the production front-line and were put in charge of factory operations. Back then, it was deemed unconventional for engineers with degrees to work as foremen on the production site instead of being assigned a post in the administrative field. They acquired knowledge through overseas training, applied it efficiently to the frontline, and made creative proposals, contributing greatly to improving technologies.[19] Also, POSCO implemented the Saint Technician (기성, 技聖) System under which special treatment was given to those whose skills reached a "sacred stage", in order to stimulate the development of the technicians' abilities.[20]

POSCO not only has secured operation skills, but also endeavored

18 POSCO, *Pohangjecheol 7Nyeonsa*, 603-604.

19 Byun Hyungyun, "Hangukcheolganggongeobui Gisulchukjeok", 131.

20 POSCO, *Pohangjecheol 20Nyeonsa[POSCO in 20 Years]* (Pohang, 1989), 668-669.

to improve the equipment. In the course of using imported equipment on the frontline, many problems arose for which no solutions could be given by the manufacturers. While POSCO was addressing the problems, it changed or improved the equipment to adapt to the conditions of the frontline. In the 1970s, for technological improvement aimed at reducing costs, POSCO simplified relevant equipments, partially changed their operation methods, and additionally installed a few devices.[21] This kind of technological improvement significantly increased the efficiency of factory operation and improved productivity, but efforts for radically improvements were scarce, based on the sufficient understanding of technologies embodied in the equipment.

As discussed thus far, POSCO's technological activities in the 1970s focused on the acquisition of technologies that had already been standardized in advanced countries. The development of technological capabilities at the time had the features of accommodating the technical system of advanced countries to a different space of the Pohang steel mill. The company swiftly applied the existing technical system and partially improved some of its components, but these efforts could neither lead to developing new components nor a new technical system. In this sense, technological activities in the 1970s are deemed to have focused on an effective representation of the existing technical system.

21 Park Woohee and Bae Youngho, *Hangugui Gisulbaljeon,* 175-189.

Technological Catch-up through Task Force Teams

POSCO assumed the imitator type of acquiring widely adopted technologies in the 1970s, while from the 1980s, it responded swiftly to advanced technological innovations by assuming the fast follower type.[22] In the 1980s, a large number of state-of-the-art equipment was introduced through the construction of the Gwangyang Steelworks, making the securing of technologies for smooth operation of this equipment an important issue. However, developed countries were reluctant to transfer such technologies, or advanced steelworks in foreign countries were also in their early stages. POSCO could not obtain the technologies it needed all at once as in the past, and was forced to independently develop important technologies.

POSCO began to drastically reorganize the technology institute established in 1977 to set up a new R&D system. This led to the establishment of the Pohang University of Science and Technology (POSTECH, 포항공대) in 1986 and the Research Institute of Industrial Science and Technology (RIST, 산업과학기술연구소) in 1987. POSCO thereby became the first Korean enterprise to build a "triangular R&D cooperation sys-

22 Shaker A. Zahra, et al. classified four types of technological strategy such as ① first-to-the-market who creates new technology for the first time, ② fast follower who swiftly responses advanced technologies, ③ imitator who acquires widely-adopted technologies, ④ application-oriented who applies existing technologies to specific fields. See Shaker A. Zahra, Rajendra S. Sisodia and Sidhartha R. Das, "Technological Choices within Competitive Strategy Type: A Conceptual Integration," *International Journal of Technology Management*, 9-2 (1994): 172-195. I applied this classification to the case of POSCO.

tem" that connected an enterprise, a research institute, and a university.[23]

While securing technologies in the 1980s, POSCO benchmarked steelmakers in Japan, who had the world's best steel technology at the time. If Japanese technological achievements were reported in official documents or through informal contacts, the company made enormous efforts to meet and surpass those achievements. In this regard, Baek Deokhyun (백덕현), who through the 1980s served as the head of equipment and technology, as well as the executive vice president in technology at POSCO indicated, "We were much stimulated by our neighboring country, who was the world's top steel maker, and to how to surpass Japanese steelmaking was the imperative problem. In particular, since Japan's technological achievements and productivity indexes were known only as end results, we had to make tremendous efforts to achieve corresponding technologies. This kind of competition with Japan served as the driving force for POSCO's technological efforts."[24] Although Japan had already begun to avoid transferring technology in the 1980s and therefore failed to directly participate in improving POSCO's technology, the country indirectly stimulated POSCO's technological development through reported information on its technological accomplishments.

In the 1980s, POSCO began to examine and analyze various documents and materials in earnest to obtain information on advanced technologies essential to technological catch-up. Based on their collection and analysis of technology information, RIST steadily published refer-

23 Choi Hyungsup, *Buri Kkeojiji Anneun Yeonguso: Hanguk Gwahakgisul Yeomyeonggi 30Nyeon [Research Institutes Never Stop Lightening: The 30-Year Dawning of Science and Technology in Korea]* (Seoul, 1995), 154-155.

24 My Telephone Talk with Baek Deokhyun, 16 November 2000.

ences necessary for R&D in all areas, such as iron making, steelmaking, control, energy, steel materials, special steel, welding, and surface treatment.[25] In 1979, the company also signed MOUs with foreign steelmakers and secured an official route of technology exchange. These efforts occurred in the form of exchanging engineers for each sector and holding briefing sessions on technology, and it was used as a channel to obtain new technology information.[26]

In the 1980s, advanced steel makers began to hold POSCO in check, and were reserved with providing information. Therefore, a method that might be called a "surreptitious glance" was frequently used in the course of acquiring technological information. For example, POSCO's overseas trainees secretly copied confidential data and photographed materials and facilities if training institutions did not cooperate actively. In many cases, they made use of personal relations to collect materials or observe facilities in order to obtain information, and this contributed considerably to POSCO's planning and development of technology. This data were effectively put to practical use because POSCO had already secured a considerable knowledge base.

In this regard, Shim Jangseop (심장섭), who served as the general manager of equipment planning in the second Pohang cold rolling factory and as the staff in charge of technological planning in the third Gwangyang cold rolling factory from 1983, indicated that his observation trip in 1982 to the cold rolling factory of the Hirohada steel mill

25 RIST (Research Institute of Industrial Science and Technology), *Iron and Steel Technology*, 8 (1992).

26 POSCO, *Yeongilmaneseo Gwangyangmankkaji: Pohangjecheol 25Nyeonsa, Gisulbaljeonsa [POSCO in 25 Years: History of Technological Development]* (Pohang, 1993), 242-243.

through personal relations contributed greatly to designing the current factory in Korea.[27] Likewise, Shin Yeonggil (신영길), who worked as an R&D personnel in POSCO and RIST from 1981, recollected that he could secure materials on continuous casting and relevant specifications through unofficial contacts, and this served to enhance POSCO's continuous casting technologies greatly.[28]

POSCO made many trials and errors in developing technologies based on technological information acquired through these methods. First attempts seldom produced successes, but repeated trials could produce desired results through failure analysis. Also, development of certain elemental technologies was delayed, causing bottleneck phenomena, but this prompted POSCO to attempt again by securing additional information. These trials and errors made POSCO engineers understand the features of relevant technologies and provided opportunities to secure know-how on technological development, thus diminishing the occurrence of problems and systematically defining the causes.[29]

To effectively push ahead with technological development, POSCO organized a task force team (TFT) to focus on managing core technological tasks. To shorten the technological development cycle and the market entry cycle, the TFT carried out R&D, developed pilot products and mass production technology in parallel, rather than in succession. Also, because the TFT often encompassed RIST, POSTECH, and other companies as well as POSCO, the team could solve problems in a more com-

27 Lee, *Sindeullin Saramdeurui Hapchang*, 149-152.

28 My Interview with Shin Yeonggil, 4 September 2001

29 My Telephone Talk with Baek Deokhyun, 20 June 2001; My Interview with Shin Yeonggil, 4 September 2001.

prehensive manner. Through this, an atmosphere was created in which appropriate and relevant groups jointly conducted R&D. While running the TFT, POSCO granted an unprecedented cash prize to any team that achieved their targets in a short period of time, and actively promoted this as a strategy, thereby triggering competition among the teams and accelerating technological development. As a result, the engineers involved had to work much harder, but this greatly facilitated POSCO's effort to catch up to its leading competitors in a short period.[30]

In the 1980s, POSCO secured technology in three ways. First, the company introduced technology from abroad and then sophisticated it, for example, the pulverized coal injection technology and the slab quality improvement technology. Second, POSCO independently developed technology because advanced countries refused to transfer technology including the extra deep drawing steel and the thermo mechanical control process (TMCP). Third, Korean engineers developed technology custom-made for POSCO, the representative example being the computerization of blast furnace operations.[31]

As such, technological activities in the 1980s, in comparison to those of the 1970s, were very diverse, but the scope of technological innovation covered nearly all fields. This can be evinced by the comparison of technological achievements shown in official records published in 1981 and 1993 by POSCO. As shown in [Table 2], the 1981 materials

---

30 My Telephone Talk with Baek Deokhyun 16 November 2000; My Interview with Hong Sangbok 23 November 2000.

31 For the detail information about these cases, see Sungsoo Song, "The Historical Development of Technological Capabilities in Korean Steel Industry: POSCO from the 1960s to the 1990s", PhD Dissertation, Seoul Nartional University, Seoul, 2002, 226-230.

described a few technological improvement cases sporadically, while the 1993 materials discussed relevant technologies systematically and comprehensively.

Division	1970s	1980s
Iron making	- Instrumentation and control technologies - Operations indexes management - Life lengthening measures - Heavy oil injection amount reduction	- Supplementary fuel injection technology - Particle distribution control technology - Blast furnace computerization - Furnace wall renovation technology - Furnace rebuilding technology
Steel making	- High carbon steel blowing pattern establishment - Slag inflow prevention after tapping - Large-scale slopping restraint - Residuals stabilization	- Hot metal preliminary treatment - Steel converter operation technology - Furnace outside refinement technology - Powder injection technology - Temperature increasing technology
Hot rolling	- Heating furnace high-pressure pipe installation - Rough rolling cylinder retainer detachment prevention - Cooling water line improvement	- Heating furnace combustion control - Size precision improvement technology - Form control technology - Online roll grinding technology - Material forecasting technology

Table 2. Comparison of Major Technological Enhancements Between the 1970s and the 1980s [Source: POSCO, *Pohangjecheol 850 Man Ton Jungongsa[POSCO's Construction History for 8,500 Thousand Ton]* (Pohang, 1981), 189-190, 213-214, 230-231).; POSCO, *Yeongilmaneseo Gwangyangmankkaji: Pohangjecheol 25Nyeonsa, Gisulbaljeonsa[POSCO in 25 Years:History of Technological Development]*, 46-54, 73-78, 101-106.]

Through these efforts, POSCO transformed itself into a world-class steelmaker. Its production yield was just about 80% in the 1970s, but it surpassed 90% by 1987. In 1992, it reached 94.4%, nearly the same as Japan, at 94.8%. As of 1992, the product output per man was 880 tons, making POSCO second in the world, second only to the Japanese at 1,102 tons. The energy basic unit was 5.29 million kcal, a little lower than the Japanese figure of 5.89 million kcal.[32] Considering all these facts,

32 Korea Development Bank, *Hangugui Saneop [Industry of Korea]* (Seoul, 1993), 89.

POSCO could be considered as having reached world-class productivity by the early 1990s. In fact, based on the development of its operation technology, POSCO has been the world's leading steel maker in comprehensive price competitiveness since the mid 1980s.

As discussed thus far, POSCO's technological activities in the 1980s focused on catching up with advanced technologies that had begun to be applied in advanced countries. The development of technological capabilities at the time focused on modeling after the technical system of advanced countries, and using introduced technologies or developing technologies aimed at securing necessary components and integrating them. This pattern was similar to the 1970s in that POSCO did not create a new technical system, but different in that it furthered or developed element technology comprised of the existing technical system. In this sense, technological activities done in the 1980s carried the features of innovating some components within the existing technical system.[33]

33 In this point, I applied Henderson and Clark's ideas to the case of POSCO. They classified types of technological innovation with reference to core concepts and components such as incremental innovation (innovation without changes of core concepts and components), modular innovation (innovation with change of components under existing core concepts), Architectural Innovation (innovation with change of core concepts utilizing existing various components), and radical innovation (innovation both with changes of core concepts and components). See Rebecca M. Henderson and Kim B. Clark, "Architectural Innovation: The Reconfiguration of Existing Product Technologies and the Failure of Established Firms", *Administrative Science Quarterly*, 35-1 (1990): 9-30.

Technological Creation of Next-generation Steel Technology

Around 1990, the global steel industry entered a phase of rapid technical change, far reaching enough to be called a "technical revolution." It was during this time that the next-generation steel technology, which made it possible to skip or directly connect previously separated production processes, began to emerge. This next-generation steel technology can be categorized into the new iron making technology and the new casting technology. The former involves direct reduction and smelting reduction, and the latter involves thin slab casting and strip casting. Direct reduction is a technology designed to produce an alternative to steel scrap as the supply shortage of steel scrap deepens. Smelting reduction is a method that reduces melted iron ore in order to directly produce pig iron or molten iron. Thin slab casting integrates the continuous casting process and a part of the hot rolling process, while the strip casting integrates the continuous casting process and the entire hot rolling process.[34]

Classifi -cation	Iron making			Steel making	Contin -uous casting	Hot rolling			Cold rolling
	Coke	Sinte -ring	Blast furnace			Heating furnace	Rough rolling	Finishing rolling	
Smelting reduction									
Thin slab casting									
Strip casting									

Table 3. Outline of next-generation steel technology [Note: The shaded parts are the processes that can be skipped or integrated.]

As POSCO pushed ahead with R&D on next-generation steel technology, investment sharply increased. For example, between 1999 and 2000, 81.7 billion won was spent on the strip casting project, and 60.0 billion won was spent on the smelting reduction project. While only about 1 billion won was spent even on a large-scale technology development project in the 1980s, tens of billions of won were spent on next-generation steel technology projects in the 1990s. Obtaining an enormous budget for R&D became a pressing task. For the smelting reduction project, POSCO managed to obtain 22.2 billion from the government, but it had to press forward with the strip casting project alone, provoking a great deal of controversy.[35]

To develop next-generation steel technology, POSCO established a new organization in the form of a project team and recruited excellent research personnel for it. This project team was a more advanced version of the TFT in the 1980s. Whereas the TFT functioned for a relatively short period, this project team was intended to function for over 10 years. Since 1987, RIST has been conducting basic study on smelting reduction and new casting technology. Also, the strip casting (S/C) project team was launched in March 1990 and the smelting reduction (S/R) project team in February 1991. These project teams had the same level position as their parent organization. The strip casting project team was led by Dr. Shin Yeonggil, and the smelting reduction project team by Dr. Lee

34 For the change of technological paradigm in the iron and steel industry, see Sungsoo Song, "Cheolgangsaneobui Gisulhyeoksinpaeteongwa Baljeongwaje" ["The Patterns and Directions of Technological Innovation in the Iron and Steel Industry"], *Journal of Korea Technology Innovation Society* 3-2 (2000): 94-110.

35 POSCO, *Jegang 25Nyeonsa[Steel Making in 25 Years]* (Pohang, 1998), 242.

Ilok (이일옥) from 1992. Most of the researchers in these teams either had Ph.D. degrees or abundant research experience.[36]

The development of a next-generation steel technology started with gathering technological information. Some of these methods had only just been attempted to commercialization, there were no obvious and definitive results, and this caused many difficulties in establishing the directions of R&D. In the case of smelting reduction, Vöest of Austria developed the coal ore reduction (COREX) process in early 1985. In November 1987, a plant with an annual production capacity of 300,000 tons was completed at Iscor's Pretoria Steelworks in South Africa and began normal operations in November 1989. In case of thin slab casting, Germany's Schloemann Siemag developed the compact strip production (CSP) process in December 1986. In July 1989, a plant with an annual capacity of 600,000 tons was completed at Nucor's Crawfordsville Steelworks in the United States, and this steelworks was striving to obtain operation technology.[37]

RIST researchers collected information on the existing situation and problems of technological development by individually reaching out to their contacts that were involved in R&D on next-generation steel technology in advanced companies. The information obtainable from developed countries at that time was neither complete nor fully reliable. For such reasons, RIST continually corrected and supplemented the infor-

36 My Interview with Lee Ilok, 30 June 1999; My Interview with Shin Yeonggil, 4 September 2001.

37 Korea Research Association of New Iron and Steel Making Technology(KANIST), *2000 Nyeondaeui Sincheolganggisul: Yeongugaebal Gwaje [New Iron and Steel Making Technology in the 2000s: R&D Projects]* (Seoul, 1990), 26-28, 58-60.

mation through laboratory tests. Unlike the past technological activities, the technological achievements of foreign countries were not obvious, which meant that a separate work was required, even when specific goals for technological development were established. In the case of the next-generation steel technology, all the basic technologies necessary for the three stages of process design, facility manufacturing, and plant operation had to be domestically established. Therefore, if an error were found in one part, then the direction of R&D itself had to be revised. The past technological activities were successively performed for each stage, but the next-generation steel technology was developed as each stage was repeated and gradually progressed like moving in a spiral.[38]

Unlike in the past, various methods of the next-generation steel technology tended to appear concurrently, enough to be called a "renaissance of steel technologies." The smelting reduction method not only included COREX, but also direct iron ore smelting reduction (DIOS), high intensity smelting (HISMELT), and cyclone converter furnace (CCF). Likewise, the thin slab casting method not only included CSP, but in-line strip production (ISP), flexible thin slab casting (FTSC), and quality strip production (QSP).[39] Among these, POSCO decided to select COREX and ISP, which were deemed to be the most favorable in terms of both technological and economic aspects. As to smelting reduction, Iscor was operating a plant with a capacity of 300,000 tons based on COREX,

38 My Interview with Lee Ilok, 30 June 1999; My Interview with Shin Yeonggil, 4 September 2001.

39 For the detail information about various methods in the next-generation steel technology, see KANIST, *2000 Nyeondaeui Sincheolganggisul*, 13-86; Lee Ilok, "Cheolganggisurui Hyeonjaewa Mirae" ["The Present and Future of Iron and Steel Technology"], *POSRI Steel Journal* 2-3 (Seoul, 1997): 21-42.

but POSCO decided to use the capacity to 600,000 tons, a volume high enough to realize economy of scale. In thin slab casting, Nucor was operating a plant with a capacity of 600,000 tons where CSP was applied and it planned to expand the capacity to 1.8 million tons in 1994. POSCO decided to build a plant with a capacity of 1.8 million tons using ISP, which required a shorter production process and was thus less expensive to install than CSP.

Around 1990, by building a pilot plant, POSCO repositioned itself to securing technology necessary for commercialization. The pilot plant was designed and manufactured jointly by foreign and domestic engineers, with the design led by foreign teams and the manufacturing by domestic teams. Vöest participated in smelting reduction and Britain's Davy Distington participated in strip casting through joint R&D. It was relatively easy to build the pilot plant for smelting reduction because Vöest had already accumulated relevant experience, but there were many difficulties in constructing the pilot plant for strip casting because Davy lacked the ability and made frequent design modifications. Davy had been recruited because leading global plant builders, including Mannesman Demag, had refused to cooperate with POSCO.[40]

After the pilot plants were built, POSCO conducted dozens of pilot operations to increase the production capacity, improve the quality, and complement facilities, and in doing so, the company worked to determine the plant specifications and operating conditions applicable to actual plants. In this process, the company developed a technical system with a high possibility of commercial use, before the plant construction

---

40 POSCO, *Jegang 25Nyeonsa*, 243-244.

project was started. For smelting reduction, the daily production output increased from 10 tons to 150 tons, while the thin slab casting secured technology designed to mass-produce cast strips with the thickness of 14mm.[41]

Based on these preparations, POSCO organized the COREX project team and the strip casting team in October 1992 to push forward with a project for constructing an actual plant. The construction of a new COREX iron-making plant with an annual capacity of 600,000 tons began at Pohang Steelworks in November 1993 and completed in November 1995. POSCO began normal operation of this new iron-making plant in December 1996, and in early 1998, exported COREX operation technology to Saldanha of South Africa and Jindal Vijaynagar Steel Ltd. (JVSL) of India.[42]

The construction of Mini Mill 1 with an annual capacity of 1.8 million tons was carried out from December 1994 to October 1996. Because ISP selected by POSCO was less technically stable than CSP, problems such as breakout of steel and poor quality were prone. As a result, Mini Mill 1 underwent trial and error for about three years before attaining standard operation in July 1999. POSCO's thin slab casting technology was praised by Mannesman Demag, and POSCO reaped the benefits of selling this technology to Hoogovens of the Netherlands in October 1999.[43]

As such, POSCO secured manufacturing technologies regard-

---

41 RIST, *Pohangsaneopgwahagyeonguwon 10Nyeonsa [RIST in 10 Years]* (Pohang,1997), 473-484.

42 *POSCO Sinmun [POSCO News]* 28 May 1998.

43 *POSCO Sinmun [POSCO News]* 14 August 1999.

ing the smelting reduction and thin slab casting methods, and exported them to foreign countries, thus paving the way for the company to grow as the world's top steel maker even in new steel technology paradigms. This process shows how POSCO has change the pattern of its cooperation with advanced foreign steel makers. POSCO received the transfer of technologies from advanced countries directly or indirectly in the past, but recently, the company has started to pursue technological cooperation with advanced firms on an equal stance. With Vöest's and Mannesman Demag's plant manufacturing technologies combined with POSCO's operation technologies, technologies of smelting reduction and thin slab casting are now being exported in the package form. In particular, Mannesman Demag, which initially refused to cooperate with POSCO regarding thin slab casting, later pursued technological cooperation with it. This achievement was made possible as POSCO has secured complementary assets.[44]

Moreover POSCO went on to propose a new idea in the process of commercializing next-generation steel technology. COREX is problematic because it requires use of pellets of 8~35 mm as raw material in order to allow smooth passage of reaction gases inside the container. To overcome this shortcoming, the company sought for a new method that could utilize fine ore with a particle size of less than 8 mm and called it fine iron ore reduction (FINEX). After succeeding in the test operations at a daily capacity of 150 tons in August 1999, POSCO began to jointly

44 For the importance of complementary assets in technological cooperation, see David. J. Teece, "Profiting from Technological Innovation: Implications for Integration, Collaboration, Licensing and Public Policy", *Research Policy* 15- 6 (1986): 285-305.

develop the FINEX method with Vöest in November 1999. A FINEX demo plant with an annual capacity of 600,000 tons was completed in May 2003, and it secured plant technology for commercialization and completed the development of operation and maintenance technology. The construction of a FINEX commercialization plant with an annual capacity of 1.5 million tons was started in August 2004 and completed in May 2007. The basic design was accomplished by Vöest, and the detailed design and construction were carried out by POSCO. POSCO produced 4,300 tons of steel a day at the FINEX commercial plant in September 2007, thereby reaching normal operation for the first time in the world.[45]

In addition, POSCO endeavored to establish a mini mill within an integrated mill (MMIM). This aimed to use smelted iron produced from the blast furnace as the primary material, giving hot-rolled steel plate in the mini mill as the end product, thus resolving shortcomings of the iron-making process that makes it difficult to flexibly respond to demand and supply, as well as that of the mini mill, which makes it difficult to secure superior quality.[46] This scheme was not realized for the second mini mill construction was halted in May 1998 with the backdrop of the IMF crisis, but the attempt was evaluated as POSCO selectively integrating diverse technological possibilities and establishing its own technical systems.

---

45 For the detail information about the process and characteristics in the development of FINEX, see Sungsoo Song and Wichin Song, "Korekseueseo Painekseuro: Poseukoui Gyeongnosilhyeonhyeong Gisulhyeoksin"["From COREX to FINEX: The Case of Path-revealing Innovation in POSCO"], *Journal of Korea Technology Innovation Society*, 13-4 (2010): 700-716

46 Hong Sangbok, "Hybrid Steel Works at POSCO: Mini Mill within an Integrated Mill", *POSRI Steel Journal* 1-5 (1996): 108-129.

As discussed thus far, since the 1990s, POSCO maintained the posture of the first-to-the market, and undertook to create flexible-stage technologies for which no clear-cut achievements were attained or little precedents existed even in advanced countries. In the development of next-generation steel technology, POSCO used components that only partially appeared in advanced countries and complemented them, establishing new technical systems. In this respect, technological activities since the 1990s transcended the level of component innovation within existing technical systems into the stage of developing new technical systems all together. While such kinds of technological activities had yet been limited to a few cases, and commercialization effects had yet to be fully realized, it implies that POSCO had started to lead technological innovation in the world's steel industry.

Summary and Implications

Technological capabilities of POSCO have been developed through the acquisition, catch-up, and generation stage. In the 1970s, basic technologies for steelworks operations were acquired mainly from the Japanese firms. Overseas training was the primary route of technology transfer, and acquired technologies were articulated through actual operation. Technological activities in the 1980s concentrated on intentionally catching up to the advanced technologies. Technological information was broadly accumulated, task force teams were constructed for developing important technologies, and the scope of technological innovation was broadened to cover nearly all fields. In the 1990s POSCO launched long-term projects based on the large-scale investments, and challenged the frontiers technology. Next generation steel technologies were promptly commercialized with proper technological choices and new technological concepts were developed.

Some implications can be induced from this paper as follows.

First, activities related to acquiring technological information, the starting point of innovations, show different features in different periods. During the stage of technological acquisition with barely any knowledge base, technological information focuses on quantity rather than quality, and is not collected systematically. During the technological catch-up stage, technological information began to be gathered systematically, and with a somewhat structured knowledge base, unofficial methods are effective to acquire actual information. In the stage of technological creation, technological information collected is partial and incomplete, so additional activities are needed to revise and reconstruct it.

Second, characteristics of technological cooperation vary according to periods. In the stage of technological acquisition, advanced countries are positive in technological cooperation, and particularly, the transfer of mature technologies is feasible. During the technological catch-up stage, advanced countries tend to avoid technology transfer, but contribute indirectly to the development of technological capabilities as they serve as the models of technological catch-up. In the stage of technological creation, the importance of technological cooperation is not necessarily lessened, but is effective only when the relevant actors secure complementary assets.

Third, to effectively pursue innovations, it is necessary to appropriately form relevant organization. In the case of POSCO, it deployed engineers with degrees in higher education in the production site and gave special treatment to superior technicians during the technological acquisition stage. In the technological catch-up stage, R&D organization was constructed and task force teams on major technological tasks were formed and managed intensively. In the technological creation stage, investments were remarkably increased, long-term project teams were formed, and high-class research manpower with new knowledge was recruited.

Fourth, some Korean firms have shed innovations under existing technical systems, and are entering into the stage of making new technical systems. For example, POSCO has begun the stage of developing new technical systems, leaving behind the stage of representing its existing technical system and components, and of innovating some components under the existing technical systems. Nowadays, the capabilities to explore and navigate uncertain technological paths, to move beyond acquiring and catching up with advanced technologies through known technological paths are required. To reveal this point, additional research needs to be carried out on the development of technological capabilities in Korean firms after the 1990s. This will lead to insight on the mechanisms of development of Korea's technological capabilities, which are still left obscure, in the black box.

Technology Gap, Research Institutes, and the Contract Research System

The Role of Government-funded Research Institutes in Korea*

Manyong Moon

Introduction

Nothing demonstrates the function of technology as the key element of economic growth better than the recent economic history of East Asia.[1] Korea has little in the way of natural resources, but its ability to effectively utilize its human resources for the indigenization, improvement, and commercialization of foreign technologies has been prominent. Generally, technological knowledge is transferred from industrial countries in diverse forms, such as licensing, importing of machines embodying advanced technology, inviting foreign expert engineers or consultants, foreign direct investment, and joint businesses. These transferred

---

* This article was published in *The Korean Journal for the History of Science*, 33-2 (2011).

1 See Rudi Volti, *Technology Transfer and East Asian Economic Transformation* (Washington DC, 2002).

technologies usually required local adaptation through trial and error, collective testing, and pilot production until they could be mastered. Such an adaptation process is a duty of the recipient of technologies; however, it needs external assistance before it is able to exercise such competence. In the case of Korea, government-funded research institutes, or GRIs, established in the 1960s and 1970s were endowed with such a mission.[2]

Though various different policies and approaches can be observed, a common factor is the processes of bridging technology gaps in East Asian countries is the significant role of the governments. Of course, the process established and carried out for it was different from other countries, and it wasn't easy to find a single model of success among these nations. As the Korean economy grew rapidly in the 1960s and 1970s, Korea's technological capabilities grew as well, fostered by the government's efforts to develop science and technology (S&T).[3] The Korean government founded a research institute, which despite being run by government funds, was a legally independent corporation. This institute performed research on industrial technology and provided the results to industries in order to assist them in enhancing their level of technology. Furthermore, the establishment of the first GRI, the Korea Institute of Science and Technology (KIST) in 1966 became a starting point of the formation of a modern S&T system in Korea, composed of research

2 For the brief history of GRIs, see Yim, Deok Soon & Kim, Wang Dong, "The Evolutionary Responses of Korean Government Research Institutes in a Changing National Innovation System," *Science, Technology & Society*, 10-1 (2005): 31-55.

3 For more information on the history of technology in contemporary Korea, see Kim Linsu, *Imitation to Innovation: The Dynamics of Korea's Technological Learning* (Boston: Harvard Business School Pr., 1997); Korea Institute of S&T Evaluation and Planning (KISTEP) ed., *Hanguk Gwahakgisuri Georeoon Gil [Dynamic History of Korean Science & Technology]* (Seoul, 2010).

institutes, administrative agencies, and other supporting institutions. Through the 1970s, the government established over a dozen research institutes in each industrial field, modeled after KIST, which was the focus of the S&T policy. It is not incorrect to observe that the history of Korea's S&T in the 1970s was fused with the history of institution building.[4]

Why did the Korean government embark on the establishment of multiple GRIs, and what results were harvested as a result of focusing national policy on bridging technological gaps? Can this policy be evaluated as having been successful enough for other developing countries to accept it as a useful model? To answer these questions, I will trace back the early history of KIST and analyze its role in bridging the technology gap in Korea.

I have divided my essay into three main parts; first, with a focus on the contract research system, I will describe the process of the establishment of KIST. Second, by closely examining specific examples, I will illustrate the actual roles that KIST played. Lastly, I will explain the reshaping of its mission with the difficulties of the contract research system. This case study is a good example of an institutional policy, and how research institutes are established in order to bridge technology gaps and create an S&T system in a developing country.

4 See Moon Manyong, "The Creation of Government-supported Research Institutes during the Park Chung-hee Era," *STI Policy Review*, 2-2 (2011): 55-65.

Birth of the First Government-funded Research Institute

Since Korea's liberation from Japanese colonization in 1945, Korean scientists had constantly requested for government endeavor to promote S&T. In particular, they requested the establishment of an advanced research institute and a central administrative agency for S&T policy. However, the government did not respond seriously to these requests until the 1960s. Following a coup d'état in 1961, a military regime took over the administration, and primarily seeking to promote economic growth, it took an active interest in advancing S&T. Despite touching on technical training, this initiative did not, however, contain any comprehensive planning for the development of S&T.

The Korea-US Summit Meeting in 1965 provided the momentum needed for the future development of S&T. During the Summit, the US President at the time, Lyndon B. Johnson, offered to send his science advisor as an envoy to Korea to explore the feasibility of US cooperation in establishing a Korean institute for industrial technology and applied sciences. Korean President Park Chung Hee welcomed the offer. This news stimulated general interest in S&T amongst the Korean public, and many newspapers began to report on topics such as the terrible research environment, the poor treatment of scientists, and the issue of "brain drain." At the time, brain drain was a serious problem in Korea, the primary reason for this being the lack of job positions that required, and would accordingly compensate for those with higher education.[5] A

5 For the brain-drain in Korea, see Yoon, L. Bang-Soon, "Reverse Brain Drain in South

significant number of scientists and engineers were filled with anticipation that the new institute would provide new opportunities in the field of S&T.

Some scientists opined that improving research environments of existing institutes that faced shortage of research funds and facilities were of higher priority. However, the Korean government argued that given the limited finances, the problems of national and public research institutes could be best solved through the creation of a brand new institute that could reform the entire culture of research in Korea. Relying on US aid, the Korean government pushed ahead with the plan.

President Johnson's offer was, above all, a token of gratitude to the Korean government for its decision to dispatch Korean combat troops to Vietnam and fight as an ally to the US. It also aimed to help Korea mitigate brain drain which was a controversial issue in the international community during that era. At the same time, this offer was designed to placate Koreans' opposition to the normalization of Korean-Japanese diplomatic relations, which was in the final stages of negotiations, indicating in a way that US assistance would continue even after the restoration of diplomatic relations between the two countries.[6]

Two months after the summit, President Johnson's science advisor, Donald Hornig, visited Korea to survey the situation. He conferred with

Korea: State-led Model," *Studies in Comparative International Development*, 27-1 (1992): 4-26.

6 Donald F. Hornig Oral History, (Lyndon Baines Johnson Library Oral History Collection Interview I, 1968. 12. 4), http://www.lbjlib.utexas.edu/johnson/archives.hom/oralhistory.hom/Hornig-D/hornig1.PDF, accessed December 2005; Henry Lambright, *Presidential Management of Science and Technology: The Johnson Presidency* (Austin, 1985), 95.

scientists, government officials, and key industrialists, and inspected laboratories in universities, industrial plants, and governmental and private research establishments. After returning to the US, Hornig presented a report in which he maintained that the proposal to set up a new institute was timely given the prospects for rapid growth of Korean industry.[7] He advised that USAID assist with its establishment in conjunction with an American technical organization like the Battelle Memorial Institute (BMI). Accordingly, the private, non-profit BMI in Ohio was chosen as a sister institute and given the role to assist the establishment and operation of a new institute.[8]

In 1966, with the aid of the US government, KIST was established as a non-profit organization. The US government granted 7.18 million dollars to KIST, and the Korean government endowed 14.1 million dollars for its establishment and operation during its first 5 years. Although KIST was established with financial assistance from the Korean and US governments, it had the legal form of an independent corporation. Park Chung Hee became the founder of KIST in a private capacity. This was mainly because the Korean government wanted to avoid inefficiencies, such as bureaucratic regulation of recruitment and accounting, which were common to its national and public research institutes. The US government also agreed on the legal arrangements, so as to prevent excessive interference by the Korean government. KIST was able to secure stable

7 Donald F. Hornig, "Report to the President: Regarding the Feasibility of Establishing in Korea with US Cooperation an Institute for Industrial Technology and Applied Science" (1965). The KIST Archive owns a copy of the report.

8 For more information about the BMI's role, see Battelle Memorial Institute, *Report on Battelle's Assistance to the Korea Institute of Science and Technology* (Columbus, 1971).

government support through the "Promotion Act for KIST," which stipulated payment of endowment funds and transfer of state-owned property. The reason why the term 'government endowment fund' was used instead of the more common term 'government subsidy,' was because they wanted to avoid arduous audits or accounting that were required under the "Subsidy Management Act." Hence, a unique form of research organization called a "government-funded research institute" was born.

KIST recruited Korean scientists located overseas to return home to serve as its core researchers, and it took on a role as the "reverse brain drain center." Because Korea suffered from serious brain drain, the scientists that KIST repatriated came to symbolize change in Korea.[9] In fact, President Park considered KIST a national symbol of "the modernization of the fatherland," which was Park's key motto, prompting him to order active support for the institute. Under the aegis of the Korean government, the institute acquired equipment that would enable high-quality research and a distinguished staff that would carry out the research, and KIST was seen as an achievement that the Park regime could be proud of.

The goal of KIST was to contribute to the development of the Korean economy through industrial research, which meant that scientific research in Korea was beginning to be understood as being closely connected with economic development. Since KIST was founded under the initiative of the US, the US government exerted great influence during its

9 According to Huang, Korea's brain-drain in 1960s was most serious among the 25 countries surveyed. Huang Wei-Chiao, "An Empirical Analysis of Foreign Student Brain Drain to the United States," *Economics of Education Reviews*, 7-2 (1988): 231-243.

early years. Hornig advised that KIST be run under a contract research system. According to the contract research system, an institute makes a contract with a sponsor and supplies research results and services to that sponsor. Basically, it meant that the institute earns its budget by winning research contracts. Hornig pointed out that BMI, which was well known as a contract research institute in the US, should be selected as the sister institute of KIST.

Why did Hornig recommend the contract research system to Korea? He mostly wanted KIST to show the rapid fruition of US aid to Korea. If KIST succeeded in solving problems in response to the demands of its industrial sponsors, Koreans would be able to justify the establishment of KIST. In other words, Hornig thought that the sponsor-led contract research system would be more effective in showing the value of KIST than a researcher-led research system. Additionally, he hoped that the US government could reduce the grant to KIST if it received enough contracts.

Although the contract research system was unfamiliar to Koreans, the Korean government adopted it to reform the attitude of researchers and industrialists on research and development (R&D). It would mean that researchers would have to do practical research so that industrialists would be interested in their R&D. Namely, the Korean government wanted to implant a new R&D culture. Furthermore, the Korean government also hoped to reduce its endowment for KIST if it received enough contracts.

The establishment of KIST became a launching point for development of S&T in Korea. The Korean government realized the necessity of a governmental agency for effectual administration and support for the new institute. As a result, the year after the birth of KIST, the Ministry of Science and Technology (MOST), an administrative office for S&T policy was founded and the scientists' long waited requests of political endeavor to promote S&T had been answered. MOST implemented many important policies regarding S&T development, including the establishment of supporting institutions for scientists and promoting the popularization of science. One Korean newspaper termed these series of events as "the S&T boom," which was not an overstatement.[10] Establishing a research institute is not a panacea for bridging the technology gap, but governmental support, including a comprehensive S&T policy, is essential and an institute could be a very effective catalyst in the process.

KIST's Role in Bridging Technology Gap

There were three types of contracts that KIST undertook: governmental projects, industrial projects, and endowment projects. Governmental projects were intended to solve problems as requested by governmental ministries or agencies. Typical examples are the development of defense-related products, such as weapons and patrol ships designed by KIST in the early 1970s, and survey projects related to government policies. Second, industrial projects were requests from industrialists to solve specific problems, mostly the adaptation of transferred technolo-

10 Moon, Manyong, "1960Nyeondae 'Gwahakgisul Boom': Hangugui Hyeondaejeok Gwahakgisulchejeui Hyeongseong" ["'Science and Technology Boom' in 1960s: The Formation of Science and Technology System in Korea"] *The Korean Journal for the History of Science*, 29-1 (Seoul, 2007): 67-96.

gies, developing new technologies, and market research. The third type was "package deal contract research," which was a bundle of government-funded projects under the contract but self-determined by KIST staff. KIST needed this governmental endowment until they acquired enough contracts to sustain it, but at the same time did not want to lose its autonomy. Finally the staff at KIST successfully persuaded the government and secured an endowment that only provided funds for research excluding operating expenses, which meant the government had no rights to be involved in the administration of the fund.

Since KIST was a research institute, R&D was fundamental to bridging the technology gap. However, there were more ways for KIST to contribute to the industry than just research. Firstly, KIST demonstrated to Korean companies that R&D could pay for itself, thus providing a stimulant to industrial research. When KIST was established, most Korean companies depended on simple imitation and old foreign technology. In other words, Korean industries had not yet developed to a point where they could develop a systemized R&D. They did not recognize any necessity for developing new products or processes through in-house R&D, and it was very rare for them to sign research contracts with independent research institutes. The staff at KIST was thus not sure on whether the industry was interested in paying for R&D. In order to sign a contract, they needed to advertise their R&D ability and convince industrialists of its necessity. Few companies gave favorable responses to research budget proposals presented by KIST and some businesspersons asked technical advice by treating a researcher to dinner without contracts.

However, this atmosphere began to change as more and more cases of successful contract research took place at KIST. Several companies at risk were revived by the assistance of KIST, and some companies emerged triumphant in commercialization of the technology developed by KIST. For example, a spinning company was undergoing difficulty due to the breakdown of imported machines, but the foreign company that originally manufactured the machines demanded an unreasonable sum of money and duration for fixing the mess. Fortunately, the Polymer Laboratory Team at KIST was able to solve the problem with less money in much shorter time than had been estimated by the foreign manufacturer. A pharmaceutical company was also able to overcome a severe shortage of raw materials thanks to KIST developing substitute compounds. This news provided great promotion of the achievements of KIST, and the number of contract signed with industries gradually increased. Of course, this was not the only factor for companies to recognize the value of R&D, but KIST definitely played a considerable role stimulating the change.

To secure continuous contracts with the industry, the first director, Choi Hyung-Sup, emphasized the significance of the first contract with the industry, which would create the first impression of the institute. He sincerely requested that researchers should never fail in the first contract with industry. In addition to granting tax exemption benefits and promoting KIST to support the industry, the government also encouraged businesses to work in collaboration with KIST. President Park instructed cabinet members to seek for ways to escalate the number of contracts. According to Stevan Dedijer, the concerns over scientific development of a top-leader are crucial in promoting S&T in an underdeveloped country, both practically and symbolically, for the general public are less aware of the importance of S&T in the growth of the nation.[11] President Park, as the founder of KIST, presented himself as a solid sponsor of the institute, mediating and solving conflicts that arose in the early stages. The president's support for KIST thus enhanced the social status of its researchers, and at the same time imposed particular responsibilities on them. In other words, President Park's patronage was a factor that helped KIST to grow stably in a short time span.

One of the most common ways to bridge technology gaps was technology transfer from foreign companies, and KIST assisted companies during this transfer process. Based on their knowledge on the technology, KIST gave professional advice on appropriate technology licensing companies, and prices for licensing contracts. After the technology transfer, KIST conducted research on how to adapt and improve the technology. For example, the Metallurgy Laboratory Team assisted the Korea Special Metal Industrial Company in selecting the licensing company, evaluating prices for the transferred technology and adapting it. After they recognized the efficacy of the technical assistance, the metal company underwent three additional research contracts with KIST.

Technical assistance in technology transfer and research on adapting technology were significant roles KIST played in its early years. In fact, although KIST did not underscore the importance of technical assistance, it gradually recognized the high demand for such activities from the industry. Back then, most Korean industries had to resort to foreign technology and direly needed practical assistance in the process of trans-

11 Stevan Dedijer, "Underdeveloped Science in Underdeveloped Countries," *Minerva*, 2-1 (1963): 61-81.

ferring technology. A sizable number of scholars argued that research organization in developing countries should pay attention to technology transfer as well as original research. By examining sample projects in Latin America, James Utterback argued that the most important role of applied research institutes in developing countries was in providing assistance for successfully transferring foreign technology.[12] At a seminar held at KIST in 1972, Glenn Schweitzer, the director of the S&T department of USAID, maintained that research organizations in developing countries should become "technological institutes" rather than "research institutes," emphasizing the assisting role in technology transfer.[13] Although the project fee for technical assistance was lower than for R&D projects, KIST became increasingly conscious of the former.

KIST's role in establishing the Pohang Iron and Steel Company (POSCO) is an interesting example of technical assistance. In its construction stages, POSCO relied heavily on Japanese engineering consulting groups and needed experienced engineers to review the conclusions. POSCO wanted to hire retired Japanese engineers, but they declined the offer, concerned for the relationship with Japanese consulting groups. So KIST intervened to assist indirectly, and suggested Japanese retirees take on non-regular researcher posts, to which they agreed. Eventually, these engineers provided advice on the construction, choice of machinery, and operation tests of equipment.

KIST did not only end up becoming a center for technology

12 James M. Utterback, "The Role of Applied Research Institutes in the Transfer of Technology in Latin America," *World Development*, 3-9 (1975): 665-673.

13 Glenn Schweitzer, "Recent Programs Related to Technology Transfer," Proceedings of the International Seminar on Dissemination of Technology, (Seoul, 1972), 126-132.

transfer, but it also functioned as a center for indigenous technological development. It developed specific products and processes at the request of sponsor companies, and sought to commercialize research products resulting from government funding, called package deal contract projects. Although companies preferred foreign technology that has already been proven in the market, they did request indigenous development depending on their needs; when a licensing company was reluctant to transfer its technology, or when they had difficulties in obtaining raw materials for foreign technology, they visited KIST for contract research.

Research requests of industry sponsors were highly diverse. In 1970, a small company brought a flexible straw developed in the US and questioned the possibility of domestic production. After signing a contract, the Synthetic Resin Laboratory Team at KIST succeeded in developing an identical product and obtaining a patent in Korea. The company also asked KIST to develop a machine for making flexible straws, eventually exporting commercial products to Europe. Similarly, there were many simple items that industries wanted to develop, especially in synthetic chemistry since Korea had not adopted a product patent system until the 1970s. If they developed a new synthetic process for imported medicines and agricultural chemicals, there was a good chance for successful commercialization. Therefore, synthetic chemistry laboratories had a host of research contracts with industries.

The Ethambutol Project was an interesting case of synthetic chemistry and showed difficulties that KIST researchers had to experience during the project. In 1970, the Organic Synthetic Chemistry Laboratory Team was asked by the Handok Pharmaceuticals Company to develop a novel process to produce ethambutol. Ethambutol was an anti-TB drug, monopolized by an American Cyanamid that was not in production despite having a registered patent in Korea. The team worked out a process different from that of American Cyanamid's patent, but the reaction required 1-nitroporpane as the first precursor, a compound produced by another American company, Commercial Solvents Company. After learning about KIST's project, however, Commercial Solvents refused sales of the substance due to its exclusive contract with American Cyanamid. So the team had to work out another complicated series of reactions that mainly utilized domestic substances, but eventually was able to obtain a patent for the process. When they built a pilot plant to produce ethambutol from raw materials, American Cyanamid tried to establish a joint venture for ethambutol with another Korean company. KIST and the sponsor company made sure that the government became aware of the injustice of the joint venture plan, and were granted a one-and-a-half-year grace period. American Cyanamid then decided to reduce the selling price of ethambutol reducing the gains of Handok Pharmaceuticals in comparison to their huge investment.[14]

The ethambutol case clearly shows Korea's inexperience in R&D and typical interference of a foreign company that owns the original technology. When a domestic company tries to commercialize new technology, the foreign company attempts to interfere through a licensing contract, a joint venture, and by dumping prices. After the controversy, the Korean government revised the "Technology Development Promo-

14 About the ethambutol project, see Moon Manyong, *Hangugui Hyeondaejeok Yeonguchejeui Hyeongseong: KISTui Seollipgwa Byeoncheon 1966-1980 [Formation of a Modern Research System in Korea: The Establishment and Change of KIST, 1966-1980]* (Seoul, 2010), 263-266.

tion Act" and secured a way to protect domestically developed technology.[15]

Thanks to the four-year protection period guaranteed by this law, the polyester films (PET films) developed by KIST were able to succeed in being commercialized, and the sponsor company became the leader of the videotape industry. The PET films were developed in late 1977 and became the representative accomplishment of industrial R&D of that period. At the time, major PET films had been developed more than 20 years ago, and the patents to these technologies had been expired. Because licensed companies strictly protected the manufacturing know-hows, the Sunkyoung Chemicals commissioned the Polymer Laboratory Team to develop PET films. Team succeeded in developing film-grade PET chips and polymerization catalysts for industrial use, and obtained competent results in optimum processing tests as well. Based on this achievement, the sponsor company started to embarked on building a factory, but controversies arose as another domestic company pushed forward with the production of PET films by importing technology by the turnkey method from a Japanese firm. This was a very similar situation to the ethambutol case. Whereas officials at economy-related ministries or conservative businesspeople were in favor of technology introduction, the S&T sector showed favorable attitudes toward domestically developed technology. After ten months of dispute, the Committee On Technology Development Review, where representatives of several ministries

15 'Technology Development Act' was enacted in 1972 with the purpose of promoting R&D in industry. Yet, the act did not contain the provision for protecting newly developed technology.

gathered, recognized the product of KIST's research as a new domestic technology that is worthy of protection. Thus, other companies were prohibited from importing foreign technology for the next four years, in accordance to the revised Technology Development Promotion Act.[16]

KIST's development of new technology requested by industry sponsor was the most powerful way to bridge the technology gap, yet development projects did not always constitute industrialization successfully. For a happy ending of a research project, the government needed to devise varied political support, including a protection period and tax benefits. Such improvements in policy for R&D were the indirect function of KIST in bridging technology gaps.

Another way for KIST to contribute to bridging the technology gap was transfer of researchers to the industrial sector. KIST possessed much excellent manpower with practical R&D experience, and they spread out to the industrial circle, effectively distributing high levels of S&T. Sometimes the researchers who conducted the contract research would move to the sponsor company for effective technology transfer. Some researchers were headhunted by the industry sector, with proposals of better benefits. In other words, KIST played a role of nurturing skilled scientists and engineers and supplying them to various fields of the economy, and this can also be considered as one of the biggest accomplishments of KIST. Although this would, in turn, be brain drain on the part of KIST, it had significant positive value in that it promoted diffusion of

16 About the PET film project, see Choi Nam Sok, "A Case Study – Development of Polyester Film," Proceedings of the 7th ASCA Conference Pre-Seminar I on the Role of Local R&D for Industrialization, (Seoul, 1979), 173-182.

advanced technology at the national level.

KIST assisted the industry in bridging the technology gap through diverse methods, including development of new technology, assistance of technology transfer, and manpower transfer. In order for a newly established research institute to deliver the results that is expected of it, the government should provide unwavering support to the institute and its major clients, namely in this case, industries. The government's efforts for the institute would naturally be linked to the comprehensive policy for promoting S&T. In other words, the new institute can function as a catalyst and a departure point for the development of an S&T system in developing countries.

President Park offered a handwritten message for the commemoration of the 10th anniversary of KIST in 1976, which read "nation-building through science, self-reliance in technology." As a token of "modernizing Korea," KIST had to undertake the mission of nation building and act as a leading institute enhancing the level of technology. That was the reason why the Korean government decided to invest huge funds in KIST and adopt the unfamiliar contract research system.

Reshaping its Mission and Contract Research System

During the 1970s, KIST became the institute that represented Korean S&T advancement, and a landmark to be visited by honored foreign guests. In 1971, the first director of KIST, Choi Hyung-Sup, was appointed the Minister of Science and Technology in recognition of his distinguished service at KIST. He served as the minister for seven and a half years, which was the longest term for any minister in Korean history. During his tenure, he drew up a plan to build a science research complex in Daedeok that would provide the groundwork for R&D in Korea.[17] With the construction of the Daedeok Science Town, the Korean government, encouraged by the initial success of KIST, began to establish a series of GRIs modeled after KIST. While KIST was a multi-disciplinary institute, newly established GRIs were to be institutes that are specialized in areas such as shipbuilding, communication technology, electronics, and chemical technology. Some of these GRIs were originally established as affiliates of KIST, but later became separate institutes. Eventually, more than a dozen GRIs modeled on KIST were founded by the mid-1970s. This is why KIST is often referred to as "the mother institute of GRIs."

Under the change in milieu, KIST tried to redefine its identity and mission to distinguish itself from the new institutes. As new GRIs chose the contract research system modeled after KIST, competition between KIST and the new institutes over research contracts and recruitment of researchers was unavoidable. KIST maintained that it would hand over short-term industrial projects to the new specialized GRIs, while KIST would take on long-term and large-scale projects that industries could not afford to develop. According to their logic, since KIST was the only multi-disciplinary institute in Korea, it would be better for KIST to focus on specialized national projects, which smaller institutes could not carry

17 For the brief history of Daedeok Science Town, see KISTEP, *Hanguk Gwahakgisuri Georeoon Gil*, 242-258.

out.

Consequently, after having had a long conference with the government in 1978, KIST announced that it would focus on long-termed endowment research projects or package deal contract research. This meant that KIST would transform into a national institute that was mainly dependent on governmental funding even though it did not formally abandon its contract research system. Why did this change arise? The official reason had been to differentiate its mission from the newly established GRIs. However, there are some backdrops behind the decision; some of them were the common factors in GRIs and others resulted from KIST's own situation.

Firstly, as a leading research institute in Korea, KIST had to comply with governmental requests including assisting in the process of S&T policymaking. Although sometimes KIST had to perform such services for the government without signing any contracts, finding government sponsors was generally easier than finding industrial sponsors. Then, KIST was not just an industrial research institute, but it functioned as an adjudicating institute whenever controversial issues of S&T arose, and it also acted as a think tank for the Park regime. For example, KIST unwillingly established an affiliate, the Institute of Regional Development in 1977, dedicated to the planning and construction of relocating the capital under the supervision of President Park. Because the aim of the institute was significantly different from the initial role of KIST, the establishment of the affiliate institute demonstrated that KIST was a quasi-governmental organization during that period. KIST's mission could not help being closely related to governmental affairs.

Another fundamental reason behind KIST's modification was

the burden of the contract research system. KIST had to adhere to the contract research system and sum allocated to the projects gradually increased. However, researchers disliked the system because they found great difficulty in maintaining contract research. Most new GRIs had similar problems since they also adopted the contract research system modeled after KIST. Why did they dislike the system?

Above all, even though industrial projects increased steadily, it was still difficult to make sufficient research contracts with industry. Since the heads of the laboratories at KIST took responsibility for searching for sponsors in addition to carrying out research and managing the laboratory, they sometimes had to spend more of their time finding sponsors. And the smooth running of the laboratories depended on the number of contracts they could secure. The top executives of KIST also had to make an effort to secure financial stability of the institute in light of the uncertainty surrounding how much funding could be obtained by contracts. Since it was difficult to predict the amount of funds, executives had to find an alternative source that would guarantee secure budgets.

Secondly, the requests of the industry sponsors for research were so varied that KIST could not fully satisfy them. Clearly, multifarious research topics created a serious burden for KIST researchers. Most researchers occasionally had to carry out research on topics that were not in their specialty. Particularly, they had difficulties in development studies, such as projects for commercialization or mass production. These kinds of projects required know-how in engineering and a close relationship with technical experts in the factories, which was not easy for researchers outside of the industry.

The 'flexible straw' project mentioned above is the most successful example of an integrated research from initial study to the development of a machine for mass production. Yet, it was not so easy for KIST to conduct all kinds of research in each stage for every project. Although the PET film research was satisfactory in the laboratory phase, the sponsor company had to overcome serious technical and economic obstacles through additional R&D before successful mass production. Setting aside the risk of failure, the company usually needs to invest large amounts of money and time for the prosperous commercialization of a new technology. Sunkyoung Chemicals, the sponsor of the PET film project was a large company and was able to deal with these difficulties. However, because of the hardship, most small and medium enterprises preferred fully packaged technology, which in turn was a large burden to KIST.

In the early 20th century, there were many independent contract research organizations in the US. Those contract institutes did not become substitutes for in-house institutes but functioned as complements.[18] The process of basic research in the laboratory transforming into a final product was not linear, and successful innovation needed exchange of experiences and information. However, contract institutes did not have adequate information, especially when related to production sites; they could not conduct all kinds of research on behalf of the in-house institutes. As Pilar Beneito argued, unless contract research is combined with in-house research, fundamental innovation is impossible.[19] The finding that the

18 David C. Mowery, "The Relationship between Intrafirm and Contractual Forms of Industrial Research in American Manufacturing, 1900-1940," *Explorations in Economic History*, 20 (1983): 351-374.

19 Pilar Beneito, "Fecundity of In-House and Contracted R&D in Terms of Radical vs.

best results arise when two kinds of research are combined also implies the limitations of a contract research institute.[20] Principally, the company had to lead the commercialization research, which should proceed with close relation to the production site. The case of the PET film shows that the significance and difficulty of commercialization research.

As we have seen, Korean companies expected KIST to function as an in-house institutes as well as a contract research institute. KIST had to conduct the entire process, from initial research to commercialization study to a plant layout, which was a unique condition to Korea that KIST had no choice but to deal with. The contract research institute in developed countries hands commercialization research over the sponsor company that possesses R&D capability up to a point. Thus the contract organization was described as a bridging institution between academic research and production research.[21] However, many Korean businesses did not have such research capabilities so they had to depend entirely on KIST, which imposed heavy tasks on the institute.

Some sponsor companies complained about KIST's research capability and some critics said its researchers were not suited for industrial research, for most of them had only worked in universities or research institutes outside of the industrial circles. That criticism seems to be reasonable, but even the researchers who came from the industry sector expressed difficulties in satisfying the diverse demands of industrial

---

Incremental Innovation," http://www.ucd.ie/economic/staff/achevalier/web/aew/pilar2.pdf (accessed November 2005).

20 Alan D. MacPherson, "A Comparison of Within-Firm and External Sources of Product Innovation," *Growth and Change*, 28 (1997): 289-308.

21 Andrew Webster, "Bridging Institutions: The Role of Contract Research Organisations in Technology Transfer," *Science and Public Policy*, 21 (1994), 89-97.

projects. One mechanical engineer at KIST who had worked for over 10 years at an American metal factory said that although he took great pride in his wide experiences as a mechanical designer, it was very tough to comply with the various requests from sponsors. And thereby, a considerable number of researchers did not like contract research with the industry, and preferred self-initiated research or package deal contracts. This situation prompted the readjustment of KIST's identity.

After the readjustment, the mission of KIST was to aim for indirect and long-term projects, although there was no change in its ultimate goal - contributing to the economic development of Korea through industrial research. KIST called its research "national project," which demanded full governmental support, for there was the necessity for research at the state level. On the other hand, it was also a strategy to upgrade its status and social image. In fact BMI, the sister institute of KIST, advised against the reshaping of the mission. However, the chairman of Board of Director of KIST replied that they were different from BMI. He said that BMI was just one of many private research institutes in the US, but KIST, as a representative institute of Korea, had to mainly carry out national projects. As a result, although KIST formally maintained contract research system, there were substantial differences between the contract research system of KIST and BMI.

The contract research system was introduced from the US to KIST in the 1960s, and in ten years, the institute modified this US-style research system. An underdeveloped Korean research environment, a series of establishment of GRIs, and the rise of KIST's national status conditioned the modification in the 1970s, and the result was a Korea-styled contract research system, focusing on package deal contract research funded by the government. At first the package deal contract research were invented to cover the insufficient contract amount by KIST, yet the invented contract projects became a major research contract due to the readjustment of its mission. Experience tells us that foreign technology should be indigenized and modified during its adaptation to a new environment. The same point can be made for a transferred foreign research system.

It was natural for KIST to reshape its mission in order to adapt itself to the changing environment. Every research institute has to interact with its surroundings and attempt to reform its identity as time passes. However, many companies, especially small- and medium-sized companies still need the assistance of contract research institutes, from simple technical advice to short-termed R&D for new products and manufacturing processes. In the early 1980s, most GRIs, like KIST, also changed their missions; they aimed to conduct national projects funded by the government. Eventually, the government had to establish another institute, the Korea Academy of Industrial Technology for technical service for small and medium enterprises in 1989. Although a specific research system is proved efficacious, diversity is more appropriate than uniformity to adapt to variety of environments.

Conclusion

KIST and other GRIs led Korean R&D during the 1970s, when industries and universities did not possess the capability and will for it. According to a report in 2004, KIST profits since its establishment recorded a multiple of 33.1 on a cost-benefit analysis.[22] KIST's way of bridging the technology gap was diverse. It is possible that its most significant contribution was in demonstrating to Korean companies that R&D could pay for itself, thus providing a catalyst for industrial research. Some scholars argue that the transfer of researchers from KIST to the industry was the most important role KIST had played to enhance the level of technology in Korea.

The early history of KIST demonstrates the effectiveness of the establishment of a research institute in bridging the technology gap in a developing country where its research system is bleak. However, establishment of an institute does not always mean improving technological capabilities of the country. To yield desirable results, governmental support is essential, which would expand into the implementation of a comprehensive S&T policy. We need to remind ourselves that the Korean government founded MOST and carried out various supporting policies for S&T immediately after the establishment of KIST. In the 1970s, a couple of newly established GRIs also became good examples of governmental endeavors for promoting S&T and bridging the technology gap. Ultimately, KIST functioned as a trigger for industrial research as well as formation of the S&T system in Korea.

In the early stages, it is necessary to set roles for each research institutes in a way that suits the actual domestic environment. Above all, they should be helpful to the domestic industrial circle in a practical manner

---

22 Seol Sung Soo et. al., "Sogwannyeongugigwan Seonggwabunseok Mit Gyeongjesahoejeok Giyeojeollyak Yeongu" ["Research on the Performance Analysis and Socioeconomic Contribution Strategy of Research Institutes"](Seoul, 2004): 39-99.

so that general society is able to recognize the value of the institutes. Rather than conducting the high-level frontier research that foreign scientists aspire for, local research organizations should focus on practical studies that are in demand at home, and the effects of which can be fully witnessed by society. In that sense, the contract research system at KIST could be deemed an effectual option for developing countries. KIST did localize the contract research system in the 1970s, but all in all, the system would have been necessary for a period of time, for conducting research that is in demand had a very significant value in reforming Korea's R&D culture. It was the key in proving the need for R&D to industrialists, and illustrating the significance of sponsor-led research to the scientists and researchers. Considering these symbolic meanings and practical effects, especially the first GRI needs to accept the contract research system in spite of its difficulties. Yet, I do not believe that all GRIs should adopt the contract research system in the same way. As an S&T system is formed, a diverse research system is necessary, depending on the area of research and the goal of the institutes. While some institutes take on long-term projects or basic research, other institutes have to comply with various requests from the industry. Although sponsor-led research definitely has its worth, absolute conformity is not desirable for the development of S&T at the national level.

Technonationalism, Technology Gaps, and the Nuclear Bureaucracy in Korea, 1955-1973*

Buhm Soon Park

There is a growing body of literature on the relationship between technology and politics, but the majority of case studies tend to focus on the central role of the state in nurturing the industrial sector of strategic importance. By introducing the concept of *technonationalism*, for instance, Richard J. Samuels has examined the social and political function of technology in developmental states like Japan, where technology is viewed as a fundamental element in promoting national security and economic prosperity—something that should be indigenized, diffused, and nurtured within the nation.[1] Some historians and STS scholars have

* In the body of this chapter I have followed the customary practice of writing the family name first for the Koreans. But in footnote I have adopted the way each name has been printed in the previous publications. To avoid any confusion, I have capitalized the family name, if necessary, like in my name. This chapter would not have been possible without Professor Youngsoo Bae's kind invitation and unfailing patience. I would also like to thank my colleagues at KAIST, Chihyung Jeon and Mina Park, for their penetrating comments. I am also indebted to my students, Young-Kyu Kim, YeonSil Kang, Taemin Woo, and Kyuri Kim, for their insightful suggestions and editorial assistance. It is my

recently sought to move beyond the notion of technology merely as part of the government's industrial policy, but seeing it as a political entity, per se. Gabrielle Hecht's study of France's nuclear program is a good example. Elaborating the concept of *technopolitics*, she draws our attention to "the strategic practice of designing or using technology to constitute, embody, or enact political goals." To Hecht, French nuclear reactors are "hybrids" of technology and politics: i.e., technology is politically constructed as much as it is put to use politically. She convincingly shows that nuclear technology was developed as a key element in defining France's national identity after World War II.[2] In a similar vein, Sheila Jasanoff and Sang-Hyun Kim have coined the term *sociotechnical imaginaries* to illustrate the power of people's collective image of atomic power in conscribing the nuclear programs of the U.S. and of Korea.[3]

In this chapter I contend that the intricacies of the politics-

pleasure to acknowledge Seung Yeon Yang's help in finding useful information from newspaper sources. All translations in this chapter are done by me.

1 Richard J. Samuels, *Rich Nation, Strong Army: National Security and Technological Transformation in Japan* (Ithaca, N.Y., 1994). See also Chalmers Johnson, *MITI and the Japanese Miracle: The Growth of Industrial Policy, 1925-1975* (Stanford, 1982); T. J. Pempel, "Revisiting the Japanese Economic Model," in *Japan and China in the World Political Economy*, ed. Saadia M. Pekkanen and Kellee S. Tsai (London, 2005), 29-44; Kellee S. Tsai and Sarah Cook, "Developmental Dilemmas in China: Socialist Transition and Late Liberalization," ibid., 45-66. See also such classics as Alice H. Amsden, *Asia's Next Giant: South Korea and Late Industrialization* (Oxford, 1989); Ezra F. Vogel, *The Four Little Dragons: The Spread of Industrialization in East Asia* (Cambridge, 1991).

2 Gabrielle Hecht, *The Radiance of France: Nuclear Power and National Identity After World War II* (Cambridge, M.A., 2009), Introduction.

3 Sheila Jasanoff and Sang-Hyun KIM, "Containing the Atom: Sociotechnical Imaginaries and Nuclear Power in the United States and South Korea," *Minerva*, 47 (2009):119-146. For the significance of imagination, see also Dong-Won KIM, "Imaginary Savior: The Image of the Nuclear Bomb in Korea, 1945-1960," *Historia Scientiarum*, 19 (2009):105-118; Maika Nakao, "The Image of the Atomic Bomb in Japan before Hiroshima," ibid., 119-131.

technology relation may not be fully captured without considering the state's administrative capacity, R&D infrastructure (manpower and facilities), and developmental strategies. South Korea's nuclear program is a case in point where seemingly unbridgeable technology gaps existed at the outset. It started in the mid-1950s when a decision was made to install a small experimental nuclear reactor under the banner of the Atoms for Peace program of the United States, further expanding its horizon to the construction of commercial nuclear power plants in the following decades. Analyzing the debates over the governance of the nuclear program, I show that the key point of controversies was often neither political nor technological but bureaucratic—i.e., it was more about the jurisdictional boundary of the nascent nuclear expertise in Korea and the administrative structure of the nuclear bureaucracy. This bureaucracy was formed not merely on paper but in action amidst the debates over such issues as: Who are nuclear experts? What qualifications are needed to claim nuclear expertise? Who should decide the future direction of the research program? Who should be in charge of the development of commercial nuclear power plants? Where should the nuclear bureaucracy be located in the changing government structure? Examining the ways in which these questions were raised, debated, and resolved, I argue that technonationalism was an ideological weapon not only for the state to mobilize the national resources but also for the emerging technocrats, the scientists-turned-administrators, to seek to find their bureaucratic autonomy in society.

My viewpoint stems from the observation that the government in the years following the Korean War lacked both the administrative capacity to run a large-scale scientific enterprise, not to mention a strong body of qualified professionals to follow through. Under these circumstances, which provide a notable distinction between Korea and other countries such as France and Japan, the government had to rely on a handful of elite scientists to build the nuclear program from scratch, while bankrolling the training of nuclear researchers and technological personnel in universities and nuclear facilities in the U.S. and the U.K. Foreign advisors came to help the installation of Korea's first nuclear reactor, but it was entirely up to the Koreans to establish a research institute and create an administrative system to support its activities.[4] Hence, amidst critical debates over whether scientists should be on top or on tap, a nuclear bureaucracy began to take a shape. Although the weak, emerging relationship between nuclear scientists and administrators in Korea is a far cry from the strong, "marriage" relationship between professional experts and government bureaucrats in post-World War II America,[5] the

4 For the early history of Korea's nuclear program, see Koh Dae Seung, "The Establishment of the Korea Atomic Institute and Its Background" ["Hangugui Wonjaryeokgigu Seollipgwajeonggwa Geu Baegyeong"], *Korean Journal for the History of Science*, 14 (1992):62-87 (in Korean); John DiMoia, "Atoms for Power? The Atomic Energy Research Institute (AERI) and South Korean Electrification, 1948-1965," *Historia Scientiarum*, 19 (2009): 170-183; idem, "Atoms for Sale? Cold War Institution-Building and the South Korean Atomic Energy Project, 1945-1965," *Technology and Culture*, 51 (2010):589-618; KIM Seong-Jun, "Development of Science Rather Than Nation: Roles and Motives of Domestic Scientists in South Korea's 1950s Nuclear Program" ["1950Nyeondae Hangugui Yeonguyong Wonja-ro Doip Gwajeonggwa Gwahakgisuljadeurui Yeokhal"], *Korean Journal for the History of Science*, 31 (2009):139-168 (in Korean) Among them, Kim Seong-Jun has paid particular attention to the unique contributions made by Korean nuclear scientists in building the research program.

5 To make a distinction between the expert-bureaucrat relation in the Progressive Era and that in the post-World War II years, Brian Balogh has coined the term "proministrative state," in which administrators proactively sought to produce professionals in the needed area and professionals got themselves involved in the research administrations. Brian Balogh, "Reorganizing the Organizational Synthesis: Federal-Professional Relations in Modern America," *Studies in American Political Development*, 5 (1991): 119-172; Brian Balogh, *Chain Reaction: Expert Debate and Public Participation in American Commercial*

Korean case can shed light on the process of bureaucratization in science and technology by an underdeveloped country that experienced a political transition from civilian to military regimes.

"Atoms for Peace" and the Rise of Technocrats

On July 14, 1959, the groundbreaking ceremony for the TRIGA Mark II atomic reactor was held at the Atomic Energy Research Institute (AERI) located in a suburban area adjacent to the campus of the School of Engineering at Seoul National University. It was not an ordinary ceremony, especially not for an institute that was less than a year old; the President, the Speaker of the National Assembly, Chief Justice, and other luminaries of the government were gathered with diplomatic envoys and representatives of the scientific community to celebrate the moment that was believed to promise a new era for South Korea, a country that had relied on aids from the United Nation's Korea Reconstruction Agency until recently. Much elated, President Rhee Syngman (이승만) said during the address that "in the future, [this institute] should make a brilliant atomic, atomic machine."[6] Although the AERI's in-

Nuclear Power 1945-1975 (Cambridge, Mass., 1993).

6 Korea Atomic Energy Research Institute, *Hangugwonjaryeogyeonguso Samsimnyeonsa [Thirty-Year History of Korea Atomic Energy Research Institute, 1959-1989]* (Daejeon, 1990), 114. The official historical volumes were published in every ten years since its inception in 1959. See also Office of Atomic Energy, *Wonjaryeokcheong 10Nyeonsa [Ten-Year History of the Office of Atomic Energy]*, (Seoul, 1969); Korea Atomic Energy Research Institute, *Hangugwonjaryeok 20Nyeonsa [Twenty-Year History of Korean Atomic Energy]* (Seoul, 1979); Korea Atomic Energy Research Institute, *Hangugwonjaryeogyeonguso 40Nyeonsa [Forty-Year History of Korea Atomic Energy Research Institute]* (Daejeon, 2001); Korea Ato-

Figure 1. President Rhee Syngman (in the middle among the three people walking out) and other key members of the government at the groundbreaking ceremony for the TRIGA-Mark II reactor on July 14, 1959. Note "Peace, Research, Power" on the banner. [Source: Korea Atomic Energy Research Institute, *Hangugwonjaryeogyeonguso 50nyeonsa [Fifty-Year History of Korea Atomic Energy Research Institute, 1959-2009]*(DaeJeon, 2009).]

---

mic Energy Research Institute, *Hangugwonjaryeogyeonguso 50nyeonsa [Fifty-Year History of Korea Atomic Energy Research Institute, 1959-2009]* (Daejeon, 2009).

house historian was hesitant to offer an interpretation of this remark, the President's message was loud and clear—the achievement of self-reliance in nuclear technology. In contrast to President Rhee's emotional statement, the three words on the banner that hung over the entrance to reactor —"Peace, Research, Power"— looked more like plain, consensual goals. Yet they were a source of contention when it came to setting priorities. "Peace" obviously denoted the origins of the nuclear program in Korea—the "Atoms for Peace" speech that U.S. President Dwight D. Eisenhower made at the U.N. General Assembly in December 1953. The following year, the Korean government received two letters of invitation, one from the U.S. government proposing the training of Korean scientists in nuclear reactor facilities, and another from the U.N. inviting Korea to the International Conference on the Peaceful Uses of Atomic Energy in Geneva. Korea and the U.S. wasted no time in taking steps to lay a legal basis of cooperation for the peaceful uses of atomic energy, and signed the Agreement in February 1956. The U.S. promised to provide grants-in-aid of $350,000 for the purchase of a reactor, while Korea appropriated a matching-fund of the same amount for the purchase of the land, the construction of buildings and for other administrative preparations.[7] It was apparent that Korea was embracing the Atoms for Peace program, even though its benign appeal to scientific internationalism and openness might have been intended to disguise U.S. interests in strengthening security and implementing regimes of surveillance.[8]

---

7 Korea Atomic Energy Research Institute, *Hangugwonjaryeogyeonguso 30nyeonsa*, 81-86, 112-116.

8 For the most recent discussion of the disguised intention of the U.S's Atoms for Peace program, see John Krige, "Atoms for Peace, Scientific Internationalism, and Scientific

This does not mean that Koreans blindly followed the U.S. lead on matters ranging from the selection of reactor type and location to the formation of bureaucratic structure. While a small group of consultants based at the University of Michigan's Phoenix Memorial Laboratory—the team that put the Atoms for Peace program into action based on its experience in non-military research of atomic reactors—provided invaluable technical advice, it was always up to the Korean government to make key decisions.[9] The Korean civil society was quite vocal as well. Some raised concerns about the conditions stipulated in the U.S.-Korea Agreement for Cooperation, and others argued in its defense. The 1955 debate between Chang Nae-Won (장내원) and Yoon Se-Won (윤세원), publicized in a series of op-ed articles of *Dong-A Ilbo*, Korea's leading daily newspaper, illustrates the diversity of opinions concerning the future direction that the Korean nuclear program should take and the ways that decision should be made.[10]

Intelligence," *Osiris*, 21(2006):161-181. See Koh, "The Establishment of the Korea Atomic Institute and Its Background."

9 DiMoia, "Atoms for Power?"; DiMoia, "Atoms for Sale?"; Kim, "Development of Science Rather Than Nation."

10 Chang Nae-Won, "Wonjaryeokhyeopjeongui Geomto-1" ["Review of the Agreement on Atomic Energy-1,"] *Dong-A Ilbo* 11 October 1955; Chang Nae-Won, "Wonjaryeokhyeopjeongui Geomto-2"["Review of the Agreement on Atomic Energy-2,"] *Dong-A Ilbo* 12 October 1955); idem, "Wonjaryeokhyeopjeongui Geomto-3"["Review of the Agreement on Atomic Energy-3,"] *Dong-A Ilbo* 13 October 1955; Chang Nae-Won, "Wonjaryeokhyeopjeongui Geomto-4" ["Review of the Agreement on Atomic Energy-4,"] *Dong-A Ilbo* 14 October 1955; Chang Nae-Won, "Wonjaryeokhyeopjeongui Geomto-5"["Review of the Agreement on Atomic Energy-5,"] *Dong-A Ilbo* 16 October 1955. Chang's articles were followed by Yoon Se-Won, "Wonjaryeokhyeopjeongui Jinui: Gwahakjaroseo Jangssisoroneul Bipanham-1" ["True Intentions of the Agreement on Atomic Energy: A Scientist's Criticism of Mr. Chang's Opinion-1"] *Dong-A Ilbo* 24 October 1955; Yoon Se-Won, "Wonjaryeokhyeopjeongui Jinui: Gwahakjaroseo Jangssisoroneul Bipanham-2" ["True Intentions of the Agreement on Atomic Energy: A Scientist's Criticism of Mr. Chang's Opinion-2"] *Dong-A Ilbo* 25 October 1955; Yoon

Chang Nae-Won, who initiated the debate that would later be dubbed as "the first press debate on scientific issues in Korea,"[11] was at that time the executive director of the UNESCO Korean National Commission. Formerly an English teacher,[12] Chang was worried that the majority of citizens, even those with considerable expert knowledge, would have difficulties in understanding the true meanings and consequences of the U.S.-Korea Agreement for Cooperation Concerning Peaceful Uses of Atomic Energy, which was initially signed by the two governments and then put before Congress for reviews. "I will give an extremely careful analysis and criticism of the atomic energy problem from the angle of political economy and from the standpoint of social sciences," he said at the outset.[13] Chang's analysis was focused on the benefits of the U.S.-Korea cooperation and the strings attached to the Agreement. The list of potential "benefits" included: having an experimental reactor; conducting a variety of research on neutrons; producing a small amount of radioac-

Se-Won, "Wonjaryeokhyeopjeongui Jinui: Gwahakjaroseo Jangssisoroneul Bipanham-3"["True Intentions of the Agreement on Atomic Energy: A Scientist's Criticism of Mr. Chang's Opinion-3"] *Dong-A Ilbo* 26 October 1955; Yoon Se-Won, "Wonjaryeok-hyeopjeongui Jinui: Gwahakjaroseo Jangssisoroneul Bipanham-4" ["True Intentions of the Agreement on Atomic Energy: A Scientist's Criticism of Mr. Chang's Opinion-4"] *Dong-A Ilbo* 27 October 1955). They are all in Korean. These articles are collected in Park Ik-Su, *Hangugwonjaryeokcheungmyeonsa: Pyeongnoneul Tonghan Cheungmyeonsa[A Side-View History of Atomic Energy in Korea: Perspectives from Op-Ed Artlces]*(Seoul, 1999) (in Korean). In this chapter I use Park's volume for reference.

11 Park Ik-Su, *Hangugwonjaryeokcheungmyeonsa*, 6.

12 Information on Chang's family and educational background is scant. According to a newly released document originally made by the U.S. Embassy in Seoul, Chang had worked in the "Kwangmyung" middle/high school in Gando, just north of North Korea, established by the Japanese military for the purpose of controlling the Koreans and training young talents for the military or police force. http://news.naver.com/main/read.nhn?mode=LSD&mid=sec&sid1=100&oid=262&aid=0000003477 (accessed on May 18, 2012).

13 Park Ik-Su, *Hangugwonjaryeokcheungmyeonsa*, 7.

tive isotopes; and being able to generate only three-day's worth of electricity with 6 kg of 20 percent enriched uranium. Chang did not try to hide his disappointment about this prospect, as he figured that the benefits would be nothing more than obtaining skills for operating the reactor and producing skilled operators. Furthermore, he pointed out that the strings attached to the Agreement—the secrecy clause, the treatment of used fuel, and the use of enriched uranium as fuel—might seriously restrict the future development of both nuclear science and nuclear power industry in Korea.

Chang Nae-Won ultimately targeted his criticism at the U.S. and their intentions. Why did the U.S. want to provide only one kind of fuel, enriched uranium, given that many other countries, including the U.K., France, Canada, and Norway, had already developed reactors using natural uranium? He pointed out that the U.S. was also keen on developing natural uranium-based reactors, as evidenced in the 1000KW reactor at Oak Ridge along with others in Chicago. He surmised with confidence that the U.S. might have a two-track plan of taking natural uranium as its long-term solution for reactor fuel, and producing enriched uranium as an export commodity. "Therefore," he contended, "why don't we establish a national policy for self-reliance in nuclear fuel by knocking on, digging up, and processing natural uranium that is ample and dormant underneath our earth in our own country, instead of *becoming a poor beneficiary-turned-consumer-turned-market of enriched uranium?*"[14] It was clear to him that the U.S. had every intention to dominate the world market in atomic energy by giving out reactors under the banner of Atoms for Peace and at

14 Ibid., 13.

the same time by sending a green, "Go Ahead!" signal to private companies. Chang thus suggested that the Agreement be modified to allow the use of "Korean-produced uranium" in the future. He concluded:

> It is my opinion that the United States can help us win the goal of self-reliance in nuclear technology and fuel processing facilities that would suit Korea and its special circumstances, instead of applying to us the same kind of principles as other countries, and at the same time assist us in becoming a country with pronounced principles of "autarky," "sovereignty," and "freedom" in the construction of nuclear power plants.[15]

It should be borne in mind that Chang Nae-Won's critical opinion came out at a time when the Korean government was scrambling to find a way to respond to the opportunities given by the Atoms for Peace program. The nuclear bureaucracy was non-existent at this point, not to mention scientists trained in nuclear fields. At the center of the government's dual efforts to produce nuclear scientists as well as to form an administrative system was Park Chul-Jae (박철재), chief of the Office of Technical Education at the Ministry of Education (문교부 기술교육국). Park was one of the handfuls of Korean scientists with a doctoral degree at that time. He studied at Yeonhuijeonmoon (연희전문) before moving to Kyoto University where he received his Ph.D. in physics, working on the crystallization of natural rubber. Since his return to Korea in 1945, Park was involved in founding Seoul National University and serving as the chairman of the Department of Physics. His career took an important

15 Ibid., 21.

turn in 1948, as he decided to work for the newly established South Korean government that succeeded the U.S. Army Military Government in Korea (USAMGIK) of three years. As "the first bureaucrat in science and technology," Park was subsequently charged with the task of developing the nuclear program, which would eventually earn him an accolade, "The Father of Atomic Energy in Korea."[16]

Park Chul-Jae was sent to Geneva for the 1955 International Conference on the Peaceful Uses of Atomic Energy, along with two others (Yoon Dong-Seok, a professor at Seoul National University, and Lee Gi-Uk, a doctoral student studying physics in the U.S.), and on their return trip, the three visited the U.S. Oak Ridge National Laboratory for a month, collecting information, articles and books, one example being *Research Reactors* published by the U.S. Atomic Energy Commission.[17] Park then met with his protégé, Yoon Se-Won, an assistant professor at the Physics Department of Seoul National University, who had been closely following Park's career path. Like Park, Yoon studied at Yeonhuijeonmoon and Kyoto University before receiving his Ph.D. from Seoul National University in 1947. Park Chul-Jae gave Yoon Se-Won what he had collected at Oak Ridge, describing the general atmosphere and sharing the major discussion points that came up at the Geneva conference. Yoon then organized an informal study group with researchers within the Army and the Air Force and junior professors at universities, all in their late twenties or early thirties of age. These members were the first group in Korea

16 On Park Chul-Jae's biographical information, see PARK Seong-Rae, "Hanguk Wonjaryeogui Abeoji Bakcheoljae" ["The Father of Atomic Energy in Korea: 'Park Chul-Jae' (1905-1970),"] *Science and Technology*, (October, 2005): 98-100.

17 U.S. Atomic Energy Commission, *Research Reactors* (New York, 1955).

to study nuclear science and engineering. The study group even conducted a comparative investigation of administrative systems in advanced countries, such as the U.S., the U.K., and France, and translated basic laws pertaining to their nuclear programs. As the volume of correspondence between the U.S. Atomic Energy Commission and the Korean government increased, Park Chul-Jae worked to create a new Division of Atomic Energy (원자력과) within the Office of Technical Education, and asked Yoon Se-Won (윤세원) to join him as its chief.[18]

No sooner had Yoon Se-Won accepted Park Chul-Jae's offer in October 1955 than he was faced with Chang Nae-Won's critical articles. From Yoon's point of view, Chang had no credentials whatsoever to discuss either the scientific or technical matters of the U.S.-Korea Agreement. In a series of op-ed pieces also published in *Dong-A Ilbo* under the title of "True Intentions of the Agreement on Atomic Energy: A Scientist's Criticism of Mr. Chang's Opinion," Yoon Se-Won contended that Chang Nae-Won had fatally underestimated the benefits that could be gained from the operation of a reactor, pinpointing the value of Enrico Fermi's small reactor at the University of Chicago that had heralded the advent of the atomic age. The significance of neutron research in atomic physics, the utility of radioactive isotopes (even in small amounts) in agriculture, medicine, and physiology, and the circumstantial reasons behind the development of natural uranium-based reactors in advanced countries—all these factors had not been fully considered in Chang's analysis,

18 For Yoon Se-Won's study group, including its members and activities, see Korea Atomic Energy Research Institute, *Hangugwonjaryeogyeonguso 30nyeonsa*, 85-86. It is also mentioned in Koh, "Hangugui Wonjaryeokgi-gu Seollipgwajeonggwa Geu Baegyeong" ["The Establishment of the Korea Atomic Institute"], 72-73.

he maintained. As far as the issue of fuel independence was concerned, he apparently stepped back. Although having said that such a view was "quite correct" and "patriotic," Yoon Se-Won nevertheless insisted that we should take into consideration the current level of our capacity:

> But the reality is that our country is not ready in terms of material and intellectual resources. . . . It is therefore fortunate that this U.S.-Korea Agreement will enable us to have a reactor. We should take this opportunity right away and make ourselves more knowledgeable in the field and prepared for constructing one with our own resources, both material and intellectual. We can then pursue developing a natural uranium-based reactor.[19]

What was most urgent to Yoon was to have a reactor installed in Korea, regardless of the type of reactor, in order to expand manpower and research experience in nuclear science. He was thus wary of "those who were ignorant of the true value of having a reactor and those who sang an ideology of scientific independence without understanding the internationalist aspects of science, the practice of international cooperation, and the progress of science and technology based on such internationalism."[20] Chang Nae-Won came close to that category, Yoon Se-Won thought.

In a nutshell, the Chang-Yoon debate was about the uncharted territory of nuclear administration and, more generally, of emerging sci-

19 Park Ik-Su, *Hangugwonjaryeokcheungmyeonsa*, 29-30.
20 Ibid., 30.

ence administration in Korea. Who should make key policy decisions? Politicians or scientists? What should be the role of a scientist-turned-bureaucrat? Where should the boundary line be drawn between politics and science? Chang and Yoon were engaged in this "boundary work" from different perspectives. Whereas Chang Nae-Won regarded science administration as a political exercise, as something that should be practiced in the interest of the nation, not just for that of science, Yoon Se-Won placed policy for scientific progress ahead of political implications of the policy. Perhaps Chang Nae-Won did not consider the fact that Korea was a much weaker partner in the nuclear negotiation with the U.S. in comparison with India and Japan, the two countries that had the technological capacity to build their own reactors and were thus worried of the possible market dominance by the U.S. Similarly, Yoon Se-Won might be naïve about the intentions of the Atoms for Peace initiative and narrow-minded about "science-first policy," as one observer of the debate noted.[21] Limited as they were in the scope of their personal viewpoints, it is important to note that Chang Nae-Won and Yoon Se-Won touched upon a matter of priority-setting in science administration—research vs. power, infrastructure-building vs. goal-oriented policy, and short-term vs. long-term planning—for the first time in Korean history.

21 Park Ik-Su, "Jaribeui Wonjahyeopjeong: Jangssiwa Yunssiui Nonjireul Bogo-1" ["Atomic Agreement with Self-Reliance: On the Debate between Mr. Chang and Mr. Yoon-1,"] *Dong-A Ilbo,* 31 October 1955; Park Ik-Su, "Jaribeui Wonjahyeopjeong: Jangssiwa Yunssiui Nonjireul Bogo-2" ["Atomic Agreement with Self-Reliance: On the Debate between Mr. Chang and Mr. Yoon-2,"] *Dong-A Ilbo,* 1 November 1955; "Jaribeui Wonjahyeopjeong: Jangssiwa Yunssiui Nonjireul Bogo-2"["Atomic Agreement with Self-Reliance: On the Debate between Mr. Chang and Mr. Yoon-3," *Dong-A Ilbo* 2 November 1955]. These articles, all in Korean, are also reprinted in Park Ik-Su, *Hangugwonjaryeokcheungmyeonsa*, 33-40.

Technocrats' Challenges, 1960-1961

The Chang-Yoon debate reveals the knowledge-first attitude held by the emerging group of technocrats at a time when the nuclear industry market was wide open globally under the auspices of the Atoms for Peace program. This group, loosely organized around Yoon Se-Won's informal study group, found its government outpost in the Division of Atomic Energy in the Ministry of Education and expanded their influence in the nuclear administration. In 1956, Yoon was selected as one of two people to receive a year-long training at a university in the U.S. and at the International School of Nuclear Science and Engineering run by Argonne National Laboratory, and he headed the Division upon his return to Korea. In the meantime, the study group drafted a bill for the Atomic Energy Act, drawing on U.S. and U.K. legislations for a general framework and on Japanese legislation for terminology.[22] The key issue the group dealt with was where to locate the nuclear bureaucracy. One early draft, which was strongly advocated by Park Chul-Jae and Yoon Se-Won, proposed the creation of a Ministry of Science and Technology to take charge of nuclear administration and other matters related for science. Another draft proffered an idea of putting the office under the umbrella of the Ministry of Education. However, the Ministry of Trade and Industry was reluctant to follow these science-oriented proposals, insisting upon the commercial and industrial significance of atomic energy.

22 Korea Atomic Energy Research Institute, *Hangugwonjaryeogyeonguso Samsimnyeonsa* , 87-88; Park Ik-Su, *Hangugwonjaryeokchangeopsa, 1955-1980 [A History of Initiating Atomic Energy in Korea, 1955-1980]*, rev. ed. (Seoul, 2002), 32.

Ultimately in 1958, after many rounds of negotiations among stakeholders, the Atomic Energy Act mandated the establishment of the Office of Atomic Energy (OAE), a cabinet-level bureau under the direct supervision of the President; the Atomic Energy Committee (AEC) composed of five Presidential appointees for reviewing and voting on related policy, budget, and laws; and the Atomic Energy Research Institute (AERI). Kim Bub-Rin (김법린), a formidable politician who had served as the first Ministry of Education, President of Dong-guk University and the majority party's congressional whip, was appointed head of the Office of Atomic Energy. Kim Dae-Man (김대만), formerly a government officer charged with foreign currency, became the secretary general. Park Chul-Jae became part of the upper echelon of the nuclear bureaucracy by serving as director of the AERI. Yoon Se-Won soon followed him as chief of the AERI's Division of Atomic Reactor.

With this bureaucratic arrangement, it was clear that the early technocrats like Park Chul-Jae and Yoon Se-Won were put to work under the supervision of political appointees and career administrators. This often caused frictions between AERI scientists and OAE administrators, as scientists were mostly graduates of top schools in Korea, who also had experienced research administration in the U.S. It was difficult for them to put up with the demand for monthly or bimonthly reports while it often took several months to have research instruments and machine parts ordered and delivered.[23] The tension within the nascent nuclear bureau-

23 On the tension between researchers and administrators, see Korea Atomic Energy Research Institute, *Hangugwonjaryeogyeonguso Samsimnyeonsa* , 91. In his oral history, Yoon Se-Won even refused to comment on Kim Dae-Man. He also found the members of the Atomic Energy Committee meddlesome. Park Ik-Su, *Hangugwonjaryeokchan-*

cracy got intensified with the April 19 Revolution, a students-led popular uprising of 1960, which overthrew the corrupted and autocratic Rhee administration. Kim Bub-Rin stepped down, and Kim Dae-Man soon followed suit. Meanwhile, Park Chul-Jae was forced to resign under the pressure of the Government Accounting Office's inspection for allegedly receiving money from companies in preparation of the groundbreaking ceremony for the reactor. This incident angered many followers of Park Chul-Jae, including Yoon Se-Won, who believed that administrators had unnecessarily blown up the case out of proportion. Subsequently, feeling that the overall research administration became slower, inefficient, and deteriorating, all the employees of the AERI wrote a letter of resignation. They put on a demonstration of solidarity by sending out the letter of resolution, the letter of petition, and the list of signatories to higher government offices and the press. Their major complaint was about the ignorance and incapacity of the nuclear administrators. Kim Yang-Soo (김양수), another powerful politician appointed to head the OAE, subsequently requested the resignation of top-level institute researchers. The blame game between the two sides continued without end while the construction of the reactor was yet to be completed. It was the "crisis" of the nuclear bureaucracy.[24]

Under these circumstances, a survey report on the status of the nuclear program in Korea caused a firestorm of criticisms, debates, and

geopbisa: Daedameul Tonghan Changeopbisa [A Secret History of Initiating Atomic Energy in Korea: A Dialogue] (Seoul, 1999), 14-19.

24 On this conflict, see Park Ik-Su, "Wonjaryeogwonui Wigi: Naebunui Suseupbanghyangeul Wihae "[The Crisis of the Office of Atomic Energy: For Moving Past Its Infighting]," *Kyunghyang Shinmun*, 10 August 1960

soul-searching. Submitted in late 1960 by Leonard Reiffel, a consultant to the U.S. Atomic Energy Commission, the report disclosed the deplorable level of laboratory facilities in the major universities and research institutes. It suggested that the urgent thing to do in Korea would not necessarily be an establishment of research infrastructure but an implementation of policy for training large numbers of Korean scientists in the U.S. or for inviting foreign experts as short-term solutions.[25] *Kyunghyang Shinmun*, a daily newspaper, rattled the public with the headline, "Operation of Atomic Reactor Far Away: Old-Fashioned Trash Facilities." *Dong-A Ilbo* gave a more detailed summary yet with a similar headline, "Korean Atomic Reactor Likely in Operation in Five Years: Facilities Are Old-Fashioned Trash,"[26] which also underscored Reiffel's advice on the need to mobilize more public support of the nuclear program by, for instance, including influential people from the business, political, and judicial sectors as members of the Atomic Energy Committee. It was not clear whether Reiffel was aware of the Korean government's fellowship program for those who sought to study nuclear science and engineering abroad, and whether he heard about the recent feuds between researchers and administrators within the nuclear bureaucracy. At any rate, the Reiffel report was a bombshell dropped on the emerging community of nuclear scientists in Korea, as it certainly disparaged the current working conditions and discredited both the administrative and technological

---

25 On Reiffel's report, see DiMoia, "Atoms for Sale?" 589-590.

26 Anonymous, "Wonjaryeokhoejeoneun Yowon" ["Operation of Atomic Reactor Far Away: Old-Fashioned Trash Facilities,"] *Kyunghyang Shinmun*, 29 December 1960; anonymous, "Hangugui Wonjaro Onyeonhuna Unnyongdoeldeut" ["Korean Atomic Reactor Likely in Operation in Five Years,"] *Dong-A Ilbo* 30 December 1960.

capacities in Korea. On top of that, the pessimistic tone in newspaper headlines was provocative enough to invite reactions from nuclear scientists. Apparently written by one of the AERI's researchers, a short op-ed piece mentioned in a metaphoric way that the problem lay in human interactions, not of machines: "we have nothing but the fact that our institute, divided into electron, nucleus, and neutron, has been engaged in partisan fighting."[27] The AERI also immediately sought to do a damage-control by pinpointing that the "old-fashioned trash" had never been mentioned in the Reiffel report.[28]

It was on this occasion that Park Ik-Su, a science teacher and writer, entered the fray. Park was no stranger to the public debate on matters related to science policy and administration. While he embarked upon his career as a college lecturer in introductory science courses after graduating the School of Education at Seoul National University, Park's interest was in the philosophical and historical aspects of science, especially its interaction with society. He gave his opinion on the Chang-Yoon debate in a series of newspaper columns, and thereafter he continued to write about science and atomic energy.[29] For this reason, Park was later called "the first science critic in Korea" and "the pioneer of Science and Tech-

27 An op-ed piece with no title, 30 December 1960.

28 Anonymous, "AERI's Clarification of the Old-Fashioned Trash Hypothesis," *Dong-A Ilbo,* 31 December 1960.

29 Park Ik-Su, "Wonjaryeokgaebalgwa Gisulhyeongmyeong" ["Development of Atomic Energy and Technological Revolution,"] *Dong-A Ilbo,* 24-29 July 1956; Park, "Wonjaro Biyagui Gijeom [Atomic Energy, the Point of Leaping]," *Dong-A Ilbo,* 25 April 1958; Park Ik-Su, "Wonjaryeok Doipgwa Uriui Gwansim [Installation of Atomic Reactor and Our Concerns]," *Dong-A Ilbo,* 16 January 1959; Park, "Wonjaryeokgyoyukgwa Daehak [Education of Atomic Energy and the University]," *Dong-A Ilbo,* 12 June 1959; Park, "Wonjaryeogui Sahoebokjihwa [Making Atomic Energy Available for Social Welfare]," *Dong-A Ilbo,* 31 July 1959.

nology Studies (STS) in Korea."[30] The Reiffel report seemed to confirm what he had in mind since the Chang-Yoon debate: the Korean atomic reactor enterprise had been initiated and driven by technocrats in a hasty fashion without proper deliberations; the nuclear program should have been discussed as part of national policy planning. In an article titled "The Agony of Atomic Energy in Korea: Towards a More Reasonable Way," Park Ik-Su asserted:

> That is to say, the installation of a ready-made reactor (i.e., the introduction of technology to society) is a matter not in the realm of experts in science and technology but, rather, in the domain of sociologists, economists, and policy scholars. Nevertheless, however, the fact is that it was decided by the one-sided judgment of a few over-enthusiastic experts in science and technology, and that politicians merely followed.[31]

At the outset, as we have seen, the scientists' rationale for accepting a small reactor without hesitation was that it would allow them to make progress in learning the nuclear fields, to train future nuclear scientists and engineers, and thereby to develop nuclear power plants with our capacity. But it turned that this would take a long, long time, Park noted. So he wondered whether, given the government's tight budget situation,

---

30 Anonymous, "Jeon Gwagijamunwiwonjang Park Ik-Su Ssiui Byeolse", ["Obituary: Park Ik-Su, Former Chief of the Science and Technology Advisory Committee Passed Away,"] *Dong-A Ilbo* 29 Novomber 2006; Song Sang-yong, "Somin Park Ik-Su, 1994-2006: Hanguk Gwahakgisulhagui Seonguja", ["Pioneer of Science and Technology Studies in Korea],"Science and Technology, January 2007, 108.

31 Park Ik-Su, "Hangugwonjaryeogui Gomin: Boda Hamnijeogin Gireul Wihayeo" ["The Agony of Atomic Energy in Korea: Towards a More Reasonable Way,"] *Dong-A Ilbo,* 7,8 January 1961.

it had been a sensible decision to spend such a large sum of money on the enterprise without considering its immediate benefit to the people. Park was no doubt an advocate of the nuclear program, and yet, he was critical of the way the nation's nuclear policy had been set up by technocrats.

Park Ik-Su's column rekindled public attention to the Reiffel report. The AERI's new director, Choi Sang-Up (최상업) wrote an op-ed piece for *Dong-A Ilbo* with the title, "Trash Dispute of Atomic Reactor," in order to stamp out any misconception about the reactor currently under construction. "A distorted criticism by laymen," Choi maintained, "would be an obstacle to the emerging research enterprise for the peaceful uses of atomic energy and furthermore make a harmful effect on the progress of science and technology in this country."[32] He was certainly mindful of Park's criticism, even though Park had already pointed out the phrase of "old-fashioned trash" as incorrect.[33] A more elaborate attack came from Lee Chang-Geon (이창건), a young researcher at the AERI. The title of his newspaper column, "Korean Atomic Energy Stays Alive," hints at how much he was upset about a layman's foray into the highly guarded territory of nuclear experts.[34]

---

32 Choi Sang-Up, "Wonjaroui Pyemul Sibi [Trash Dispute of Atomic Reactor]," *Dong-A Ilbo, 12* January 1961.

33 Park Ik-Su, "The Agony of Atomic Energy in Korea." It is likely that Park's other columns written in 1959-1960 would also have made Choi and other nuclear scientists uncomfortable. Park Ik-Su, "Baljeonwonjaroui Doip Munje [The Problem of the Introduction of Reactor]," *Dong-A Ilbo,* 26 September 1959; Park Ik-Su, "Hanguk Wonjaryeok Saeobui Jaegeomto [Reexamination of the Atomic Energy Enterprise in Korea]," *Dong-A Ilbo,* 4 August 1960; Park, "Wonjaryeogwonui Wigi: Naebunui Suseupbanghyangeul Wihayeo" ["The Crisis of the Atomic Energy Research Institute,"] *Dong-A Ilbo,* 10 August 1960.

34 Lee Chang-Geon, "Hangugwonjaryeogeun Saraitda: Park Ik-Su ssiui 'Hangugwonja-

Lee Chang-Geon was indeed a stellar example of the recently carved-out path for elite nuclear scientists. A graduate of the Electrical Engineering Department of Seoul National University, Lee joined Yoon Se-Won's study group where he was introduced to the field of nuclear science and engineering.35 In 1957 he was selected as one of the seventeen "atomic research fellows" to study either in the U.S. or U.K for one or two years. This fellowship program, run by the Korean government's Division of Atomic Energy, was indeed a crucial means to produce a number of high-quality scientists. The International Atomic Energy Agency (IAEA), the U.S. International Cooperation Agency (ICA), and other international organizations provided support for this study-abroad program, and yet a majority of funding came from the Korean government. The program began in 1956, and by 1963, the number of fellows reached 189, 125 of whom were government-supported.36 Lee Chang-Geon became one of the six Korean trainees at the U.S. Argonne National laboratory in 1959, and on his return trip, Lee additionally received a two-month training at the General Atomic, the company that had just sold its TRIGA Mark-II reactor to Korea.37 He also earned an

ryeogui Gomineul Bakham" ["Korean Atomic Energy Stays Alive: A Rebuttal to Mr. Park Ik-Su's 'The Agony of Atomic Energy in Korea'"] *Dong-A Ilbo,* 19 January 1961.

35 The members of the study group self-taught one another with Raymond Murray, *Introduction to Nuclear Engineering* (New York, 1957). On Lee's early career, see Lee Suk-Woo, "Daehanminguk Wonjaryeok Ppurireul Chajaseo" ["In Search for the Roots of Atomic Energy in Korea-2,] *Wonjaryuck Shinmun,* 19 January 2010.

36 Korea Atomic Energy Research Institute, *Hangugwonjaryeogyeonguso Samsimnyeonsa* , 110-112; Koh, "The Establishment of the Korea Atomic Institute," 77-78. The government funding continued until 1970. According to Lee Chang-Geon, most U.K. trainees were government-supported, whereas the U.S. trainees were supported by the IAEA or ICA. See Park, *Hangugwonjaryeokchangeopbisa*, 336-340.

37 Anonymous, "Hanguk Gwahakja Yungmyeonge-do Suryojeung" "[Certificates to Six Korean Scientists]," *Kyunghyang Shinmun,* 30 May 1959.

official certificate for operating the TRIGA reactor by passing the U.S. Atomic Energy Commission's examination. Proud of the first generation of Korean nuclear scientists, Lee Chang-Geon recalled their contributions in the installation of the reactor in Korea:

> We, full of patriotism, conducted a spy operation. In principle, we just had to watch with our arms folded and received the key, because the General Atomic was in charge of installing the reactor and the Homes and Narver overlooked the construction of the surrounding facility. But we participated in all the installation processes including the one for the reactor core. There was no way to fix problems should they occur, because the contract did not stipulate we be given the design blueprints. Therefore, we carried out a spy operation of copying the drawings or taking pictures of them when the company employees were out for lunch or went home.[38]

An elite scientist armed with pride, patriotism, and passion, Lee Chang-Geon found in Park Ik-Su's column not only simple factual mistakes, such as the description of Reiffel's official position, but also serious misperceptions about the governance of science and technology. Lee wondered, "Why could scientists not make a decision on the matter of science, and why should the introduction of reactor be handled by sociologists, economists, and other policy scholars, not by scientists and engineers with expertise in that field?" He disparaged Park's standpoint as "laughable" and "full of danger" of putting scientists and engineers

38 Lee, "Daehanminguk Wonjaryeok Ppurireul Chajaseo".

Figure 2. While a cadre of Korea's elite nuclear scientists was trained abroad, the International Atomic Energy Agency offered on-site training opportunities for dealing with radioactive isotopes using its mobile facility. This picture was taken in 1960. [Source: Korea Atomic Energy Research Institute, *Forty Years' History of KAERI in Pictures* (Daejeon: KAERI, 2000).]

subservient to politicians and others who had nothing to do with this field. Instead of talking about a "reasonable way" with no practical suggestions, he contended, laymen like Park should take notice of the real, hard way that the nuclear scientists of his generation strove to open the age of atomic energy for Korean people. In an inflamed tone, he said:

> No matter what others would say, we have one belief. Like a barley seed that should be perished in order to bear fruits, we would like to live a short yet thick life rather than a long and thin one, even if excessive exposure to radioactivity might have our life shortened, make our body deformed, and affect our descendants. And there is one solace in that we can be the fathers of atomic seeds, even if we, after marriage, might

> have our children in peril because of becoming irradiated with radioactivity. Among the 'agonies of atomic energy in Korea,' the most serious and harmful is the one caused by those laymen, non-specialists, who are misleading the public.[39]

Lee Chang-Geon had ample reason to underscore personal sacrifice made on the part of nuclear scientists like him. A number of atomic research fellows decided not to return to Korea or opted to work instead in other areas of study. The risks of exposure to radioactive materials were also well publicized with the 1954 incident of *Fukuryu Maru* (Lucky Dragon No. 5), a Japanese fishing boat whose crewmen suffered from the radiation in the ashes of the U.S. nuclear test conducted on Bikini Island.[40]

Lee Chang-Geon's remark did not go unnoticed by Park Ik-Su, who saw in it not only a lofty spirit of self-sacrifice and resolve—which sounded like *Yamato-Damashii* (大和魂) that had inspired the Japanese military special units like the *Kamikaze*—but also a "dangerous ideology of blind devotion and ignorant enthusiasm." He was bewildered and concerned. To Park, a reasonable way of developing the nuclear energy program in Korea could be found not in this "one-sided enthusiasm

39 Lee, "Hangugwonjaryeogeun Saraitda."

40 For the problem of foreign-trained fellows not returning to Korea, see Korea Atomic Energy Research Institute, *Hangugwonjaryeogyeonguso 30nyeonsa* , 111-112; Koh, "The Establishment of the Korea Atomic Institute," 77-78. Among the 237 trainees between 1955 and 1964, for instance, only 150 returned (66%); and among those who returned, there were also scientists who went back abroad or found jobs in fields other than the nuclear sciences. For the ways in which the Bikini incident raised public awareness of the danger of nuclear tests in Japan in particular, see Masakatsu Yamazaki, "Nuclear Energy in Postwar Japan and Anti-Nuclear Movements," *Historia Scientiarum*, 19 (2009): 132-145.

and belief" but in the "recognition of reality" in which the entire society should live and develop together.[41]

Behind this war of words between Park Ik-Su and Lee Chang-Geon was the issue of nuclear governance in Korea. While Park maintained that policy for the nuclear program should be discussed not merely as part of science policy but as part of the nation's social, economic, political, and military policy, Lee underlined the technical nature of nuclear governance that would definitely require expert knowledge. In this sense, the Park-Lee debate was a déjà vu of the one between Chang Nae-Won and Yoon Se-Won. An important distinction in this debate was the level of confidence that the nuclear technocrats had attained over the past five years; they had been both administrators and beneficiaries of the high-cost fellowship program; they had been deeply involved in the decision-making processes for the reactor type and the installation site; and they had received strong moral backing from President Rhee Syngman, filling key government positions.

But the rise of nuclear technocrats had its downside, too. Within the tripartite structure of nuclear bureaucracy—the Office of Atomic Energy (for general administration), the Atomic Energy Committee (for overall supervision), and the Atomic Energy Research Institute (for research)—the technocrats had to learn how to work side-by-side with political appointees and traditional bureaucrats, and how to deal with seemingly unfair administrative treatments in such matters as wages, promotions,

41 Park Ik-Su, "Hanguk Wonjaryeoksaeobeun Eotteoke Salgeonninga?" ["How Will the Korean Atomic Energy Enterprise Live?"] *Dong-A Ilbo,* 28 January 1961.

and appointments.[42] For this reason, Lee Chang-Geon's reply to Park Ik-Su was also a technocrat's criticism in disguise of the non-expert administrators within the nuclear bureaucracy. By the time the Reiffel report was released, the tension between new technocrats and old administrators had already boiled up. This local, institutional setting was crucial to understanding the invocation of nationalism by the technocrats.

The Nuclear Bureaucracy under the Military Regime

The political space in which nuclear scientists could contest for a technocracy was rather short-lived. In 1961, the May 16 military coup not only altered the direction of national policy by placing utmost emphasis on the development of a self-reliant economy but also reconfigured the state-society relations by considerably weakening societal autonomy. As a result, a *developmental autocracy* emerged in Korea.[43] This new environment was a mixed bag to nuclear technocrats. On the one hand,

42 For this kind of administrative problem, see Park, *Hangugwonjaryeokchangeopsa*, 113-115.

43 There is a vast literature on the development of Korean economy under the military regime. For the U.S.'s role in the emergence of development autocracy and Korea's adaptation to the American influence, see Gregg Brazinsky, *Nation Building in South Korea* (Chapel Hill, N.C., 2007); Park Tae-Gyun, *Wonhyeonggwa Byeonnyong: Hanguk Gyeongjegaebalgyehoegui Giwon [Archetype and Metamorphosis: The Origins of Korea's Economic Development Plans]* (Seoul, 2007). On the era of Park Chung Hee, e.g., see Byung-Kook Kim and Ezra F. Vogel, ed., *The Park Chung Hee Era: The Transformation of South Korea* (Cambridge, M.A., 2011); Hyung-A Kim and Clark W. Sorensen, eds., *Reassessing the Park Chung Hee Era, 1961-1979: Development, Political Thought, Democracy, Cultural Influence* (Seattle, 2011).

the military government valued science and technology as an engine for the nation's economic development, creating an all-around research institute in 1966 (the Korea Institute of Science and Technology), and establishing the Ministry of Science and Technology in the following year.[44] On the other hand, the government's support of science and technology came to be more goal-oriented than open-ended, and strongly conscribed to the needs of industrialization. "Do science," rather than "study science" or "learn science," was the motto of the day, as it appeared time and again in President Park Chung Hee's addresses.[45] This "economic translation of science and technology" led to an uplifting of the social recognition of scientists and engineers as key partners of the nation-building enterprise.[46] And yet, there was a price to pay for this partnership with the military government: taking a subservient position to economic planners.

The changes in the nuclear bureaucracy illustrate the new relationship being forged between science and government under the military regime. First of all, the shake-up of the bureaucracy effectively put an

44 Moon Manyong, *Hangugui Hyeondaejeok Yeonguchejeui Hyeongseong : KISTUi Seollipgwa Byeoncheon, 1966~1980 [The Formation of Korea's Modern Research System: The Establishment and Changes of KIST, 1966-1980]* (Seoul, 2010); Moon Manyong, "Park Chung Hee Sidae Damhwamuneul Tonghae Bon Gwahakgisuljeongchaegui Jeongae" ["A Discourse Analysis of Science and Technology during the Park Chung Hee Era,"] *Korean Journal for the History of Science*, 34(2011):75-108. Moon has pointed out that it took a few years for the Park Chung Hee administration to embrace science and technology as the foundation for the economic development.For a more detailed discussion of science and technology policy in the 1960s, see Hong Sungjoo, "The Formation of a Science and Technology Policy in South Korea and Its Administrative System: 1945-1967," Unpublished Ph.D. Thesis, Seoul National University, Seoul, 2010.

45 Moon, "A Discourse Analysis," 89-95.

46 Kim Geun Bae, "Gwahakgisuripgugui Haebudo: 1960Nyeondae Gwahakgisul Jihyeong" ["An Anatomical Chart of Establishing the Scientific and Technological State: The Topography of Science and Technology in South Korea in the 1960s,"] *Yuksa-Bipyung*, 85 (2008):236-261.

end to unprecedented open-rebellions of rank-and-file researchers against their administrators. Head of the Office of Atomic Energy was replaced with another political appointee, Oh Won-Sun (오원선), a medical officer (captain) of the Navy. In his administrative capacity, Oh carried out a drastic purge of the AERI by firing its director and two division chiefs, including Yoon Se-Won, as part of the government-initiated general cleanup of high-ranking civil service employees, which was a means of restoring order in the institute. He then forced all members of the Atomic Energy Committee to resign—members who were some of the earliest members or former directors of the AERI.[47] Gone were not only founding fathers of the Korean nuclear bureaucracy but also their sense of self-ruling and ambition for bureaucratic autonomy.

Two people soon emerged as key players in the newly manned nuclear bureaucracy: Choi Hyung-Sup (최형섭) as the AERI's director (1962-63, 1964-66) and Park Ik-Su as a standing member of the AEC (1963-72). The appointment of Choi was controversial yet anticipated. A Ph.D. in metallurgical engineering from the University of Minnesota, Choi returned to Korea in 1959 and decided to work for a private company that produced auto parts, realizing that he would not be able to pursue his research interests in either university laboratories or national institutes. A few months before the outbreak of the military coup in 1961, he was offered the highest civil service position at the AERI, the same rank as the director's. This offer in and of itself became a source of discontent among the AERI's scientists, especially because it had been widely regarded as

47 Korea Atomic Energy Research Institute, *Hangugwonjaryeogyeonguso Samsimnyeonsa* , 91-92.

Figure 3. General Park Chung Hee (7th from the left) visits the reactor facility in November 1962. On his left (a man with his hand up) is AERI's director, Choi Hyung-Sup. Head of the Office of Atomic Energy, Oh Won-Sun (3rd from the left), also attends in his Navy suit. [Source: Korea Atomic Energy Research Institute, *Forty Years' History of KAERI in Pictures* (Daejeon, 2000).]

the one that Yoon Se-Won should take in time. Although Choi accepted the offer, he could not start his job at the AERI right away, mindful of the opposition from below and also being asked to work for the Ministry of Trade and Industry on a temporary basis for the project of starting up the steel industry in Korea. Eventually it took more than a year for Choi to work for the AERI as its director. While he did not carry common denominators that could easily be found among the first-generation nuclear scientists—e.g., participating in Yoon Se-Won's study group, being selected as a prestigious atomic fellow, and earning a certificate to operate a nuclear reactor—Choi Hyung-Sup had one thing that they all lacked: the full, enthusiastic support from the OAE's head and other military men working in the key positions of the government. The close working relationship that he had built with the military government during his tenure at the AERI paved a way for his future career as the first director of the Korea Institute of Science and Technology (1966-1971) and subsequently as the Minister of Science and Technology (1971-1978), which earned him an accolade, "the Father of Science and Technology in Korea."[48]

Park Ik-Su's rise in the nuclear bureaucracy was less heralded than Choi Hyung-Sup's, but he was equally influential, moving behind the scene. Not long after the military coup, Park received an unexpected offer from Oh Won-Sun to work as his informal advisor for nuclear administration.[49] Park Ik-Su's engagement in public debates over nuclear issues had earned him a considerable degree of reputation as a thoughtful science critic, and his position as an outsider appeared to make him an ideal man to look into the current problems within the nuclear bureaucracy, such as the lack of leadership, favoritism rooted in personal relations and educational backgrounds, and the tension between researchers and administrators. Park was then involved in making the decisions for the

---

48 "Hanguk Gwahakgisurui Abeoji 'Choi Hyung-Sup Janggwan'eul Asinayo? ["Do You Know 'Minister Choi Hyung-Sup,' the Father of Science and Technology in Korea?"] http://www.etnews.com/news/economy/education/2509783_1491.html. For scholarly studies of Choi Hyung-Sup, see Yum Jae-Ho, "Gwahakgisurui Jeondosa: Choehyeongseop Ron,[Missionary of Science and Technology: On Choi Hyung-Sup]," in *Jeonhwansidaeui Haengjeong-ga: Hangukhyeong Jidojaron [Administrators in the Transitional Period: On Korean-Style Leaders]* (Seoul, 1994), 103-134; Kang Mi Hwa, "Choi Hyung Sup's Science and Technology Policy Theory for Development Countries," *Korean Journal for the History of Science*, 28(2006): 297-328.

49 The information in this paragraph is drawn from Park's autobiographical essay. Park Ik-Su, "Wonjaryeokgwa Na [Atomic Energy and I]," in Park, *Hangugwonjaryeokchangeopbisa*, 354-384.

cleanup of the high echelon of the OAE and the AERI. Subsequently, upon Oh Won-Sun's recommendation, Park Ik-Su moved on to work as the science advisor for the chief of the Korea Central Intelligence Agency, in which capacity he dealt with classified information like the status of science and technology in North Korea and other matters that might have had direct ramifications upon the nation's science administration. For instance, he prepared a manuscript for a presentation under the title, "Atomic Energy in the World and in Korea" at a special session following the ceremony at the start of 1962. This presentation turned out to be instrumental in the creation of the Radiation Medical Institute as a separate entity from the AERI. As Park recalled, Oh Won-Sun expressed special thanks to him:

> In fact, when I took office as head of the OAE [in 1961], I thought about what project would fit well with the government's 5-year planning for economic development. I came up with an idea of establishing the Radiation Medical Institute after receiving a brief on the medical use of radioactive isotopes. I worked hard to convince the Prime Minister, the Minister of Economic Planning, and members of the Supreme Council for National Reconstruction, but it was rather all in vain. But the presentation at this special session made my dream come true. Your effort was crucial.[50]

Not surprisingly, in 1963, Oh Won-Sun appointed Park Ik-Su as one of the two standing members of the Atomic Energy Committee at

50 Ibid., 363-364.

the highest civil-service rank. Park was only 39 years old.

The organization of the AERI underwent a major change in October 1961, several months before Choi Hyung-Sup took office as its head: it went from its three-division (atomic reactor, basic research, and radioactive isotope) to a six-laboratory structure (physics, chemistry, biology, atomic reactor engineering, electrical engineering, and health physics).[51] This discipline-oriented organization, which would remain intact until 1973, was clearly a reflection of what the early nuclear scientists had in mind regarding the nuclear program, i.e., an all-around scientific endeavor. The reality was, however, that the AERI under Choi Hyung-Sup's leadership—and with administrative support from Oh Won-Sun and Park Ik-Su—took a practical turn, paying more attention to medical, agricultural, and industrial uses of radioactive materials, not to mention potential military applications in mind. The Radiation Medical Institute was established in 1963, growing out of a laboratory installed within the AERI in the previous year. The Radiation Agricultural Institute came into being in 1966 in the same fashion.[52] This development was generally seen as a sign of the AERI's institutional stature being weakened rather than augmented, as one nuclear engineer has recalled: "After a decade of the AERI in operation, it was beginning to lose its original glory with the fragmentation of the research institute into Radiation Medical Institute and Radiation Agricultural Institute."[53]

---

51 On the AERI's organizational structure and research activities in the 1960s, see Korea Atomic Energy Research Institute, *Hangugwonjaryeogyeonguso Samsimnyeonsa* , 103-112.

52 On Oh's and Park's administrative support, see Park, "Atomic Energy and I," 365-368.

53 Byung-Koo Kim, *Wonjaryeokbidangil: Wonjeongisurui Guksanhwa [Nuclear Silk Road: The "Koreanization" of Nuclear Power Technology]* (Scotts Valley, CA, 2011).

It was an irony that the more the nuclear agency aligned itself with national goals that were set by the military regime, the greater support it received from the government but less likely it could build its bureaucratic autonomy. This irony manifested itself most forcefully in the development of the government endeavor to construct nuclear power plants. The feasibility of this project had been discussed from the start of the Atoms for Peace program in Korea, but it was under the military government that the idea was seriously explored. The Office of Atomic Energy took an initiative in 1962 by organizing a task force team (원자발전대책위원회) in order to examine the prospects of energy needs in Korea, the significance of nuclear power in the world's energy market, and the candidate sites for the construction of power plants. While the OAE's study was well underway, the IAEA also sent technical consultants to Korea on three different occasions to provide advice on the selection of the reactor type, the maximum power capacity, and the site of the plant.[54] The military government stepped up its effort in 1965 by dissolving the OAE's task force team and replacing it with the Presidential Committee For The Nuclear Power Plant Planning (원자력발전계획 심의위원회), which was made up of government officials from the Economic Planning Board, the Ministry of Trade and Industry, the Ministry of Construction, and the Office of Atomic Energy, and also university professors and representa-

54 The IAEA reports that came out from the first two visits are: "Report of IAEA Mission to Korea" (1963) and "Siting Aspects of a Nuclear Power Reactor in the Republic of Korea" (1965). The IAEA team made a third visit in 1967. For the IAEA's activities in Korea, see Korea Atomic Energy Research Institute, *Hangugwonjaryeogyeonguso Samsimnyeonsa* , 128-135. Lee Chang-Geon, a member of the OAE's task force team, was deeply involved in the study of candidate sites. See Lee Chang-Geon, "Naui Wonjaryeok Hoego" "[My Recollections of Atomic Energy]," in Park, *Hangugwonjaryeokchangeopbisa*, 323-353.

tives from state-run companies like the Korea Electric Company (KECO, later renamed Korea Electric Power Corporation). Appointed as chairman of the committee, Park Ik-Su teamed up with two researchers from the AERI, one of whom was Lee Chang-Geon, his counterpart in the previous debate, for a tour on nuclear power plants and financial companies in North America and Europe to assess merits of various reactor types and explore financial support.[55] It is interesting to notice a sea-change in Lee's perception of the role of a layman like Park. Lee Chang-Geon said:

> The investigative team consisted of Park Ik-Su, chairman of the Presidential committee for the nuclear power plant planning; Lee Young-Jae, chief of the physics laboratory at the AERI; and Lee Chang-Geon, a researcher of the atomic reactor laboratory. This heterogeneous team was seen as a best set-up to gather opinions from diverse fields. First of all, Lee Young-Jae was a physicist trained in the U.K., thus favoring the gas-cooled nuclear reactor. In comparison, Lee Chang-Geon, a U.S.-trained engineer, preferred the light-water type. He was a junior researcher in comparison to the other members, and yet was selected as a team member because of his ample experience in producing various reports on technical assessment and economic feasibility of nuclear reactors. Park Ik-Su, a chemistry major, was appointed the team leader because he was believed to bring a fair conclusion from a neutral position between the two researchers—i.e., an advocate of the gas-cooled reactor and that of the light-water reactor, a senior-level researcher and a junior-level one, a scientist and an engineer, a power broker and a

55 On Park's activities as the committee chair, see Park, "Atomic Energy and I," 369-371.

> non-power broker, a man with no practical experience and a man with the experience.[56]

The committee's final report submitted in December 1967 made a cautious conclusion that the light-water type would be preferable from the economic standpoint, but that its dependence upon enriched uranium, a strategically important material, should be resolved through political and diplomatic efforts.

The significance of the committee report of 1966 was eclipsed by the deterioration of the nuclear bureaucracy's standing in the government. The Office of Atomic Energy lost its cabinet-level status that year, and was supervised by the newly established Ministry of Science and Technology (MOST). The Atomic Energy Committee was also divested of its independent function of reviewing nuclear administration, but remained as a standing committee under MOST, the Minister of Science and Technology serving as its Chairman. The OAE office space in downtown Seoul had to be vacated for the MOST; it then found a new home on AERI grounds in the suburban area.[57]

None was more devastating to the OAE, as the foremost nuclear agency in Korea, than the decision to put the Korea Electric Company in charge of the nuclear power plant enterprise. This decision came at the heels of the 1967 committee report, which raised a question concerning what kind of an administrative system would be most appropriate

56 Lee, "Naui Wonjaryeok Hoego," 344-345.

57 See Korea Atomic Energy Research Institute, *Hangugwonjaryeogyeonguso 30Nyeonsa*, 127-128.

for pushing forward with the enterprise. The report recommended the establishment of a separate bureau to exclusively deal with both the production of electrical power and the development of nuclear reactors and fuel-cycle technologies. The OAE interpreted this recommendation as the creation of a new division under its umbrella or the overhaul of the OAE-led nuclear bureaucracy. The OAE's future plan was to take charge of the power plant enterprise by creating a new state-run organization like the United Kingdom Atomic Energy Authority or the Commissariat à L'Énergie Atomique (CEA) of France. Meanwhile, the Korea Electric Company (KECO) had been in preparation for this enterprise by establishing a division dedicated to nuclear power in 1966. The KECO's contention was that the production of electricity belonged to its business, regardless of the energy source.[58]

In February 1968, the military government organized a new Presidential committee (원자력발전추진위원회) in order to make final decisions on the reactor type and other jurisdictional issues. Unlike the previous committee that had been geared toward the investigation of candidate reactors and administrative systems, this committee was intended to put an end to all the deliberations and debates of the past few years. The Deputy Prime Minister was appointed its chairman to work with other high-ranking government officials like the Minister of Trade and Industry and the Minster of Science and Technology. Heads of the two operational bodies, the Office of Atomic Energy and the Korea Electric Company, were also included in the committee. Park Ik-Su, albeit serving in the committee, was rather suspicious of the political nature of the committee,

58 Ibid., 134-135.

for it could cause a drastic change in the nuclear bureaucracy in terms of its lawful prerogatives and administrative structure.[59] In defense of the standpoint of the MOST, Park wrote an op-ed piece for *Dong-A Ilbo*, in which he asserted the multi-purposefulness of the nuclear enterprise, implying that it should be regarded as more than just a means of production of electricity. Park mentioned the short history of nuclear research in Korea, for which the limited number of nuclear experts would better be managed by one administrative system rather than through competition between a government agency and a utility company. Therefore, he argued, Korea was not yet ready to follow the precedents set by other countries like Japan and the U.S., where the nuclear power plants tended to be privatized. He warned: "Ultimately, this issue should be decided in terms of high-level policy consideration, and yet we are not free from the characteristics of underdeveloped countries where power and politics are everything. I earnestly wish, however, that the decision on this issue will not be made unwisely under political pressure."[60] In response to Park Ik-Su's article, Yook Jong-Chul, a professor of Hanyang University and one of the early atomic fellows, wrote in favor of the Korea Electric Company's position. Yook reiterated here the world-wide trend that separated the government agency's supervision and regulation from the state-run or private company's construction and management of nuclear power plants. He found it unreasonable to use a 500 MW-level reactor for both

---

59 Ibid., 134; Park, "Atomic Energy and I," 371-372. Park wondered why this committee had to be formed under the Prime Minister, as the nuclear project had mostly been out of political interests.

60 Park Ik-Su, "The Standpoint of the Ministry of Science and Technology," *Dong-A Ilbo*, 17 Feburary 1968 (in Korean).

Figure 4. The groundbreaking ceremony of the first nuclear power plant in Kori, a Southeastern coast, on March 19, 1971. The power plant began its operation in 1978. A huge crowd and the presence of military men are noticeable, unlike the scene of the groundbreaking ceremony of the first nuclear reactor back in 1959. [Source: Korea Atomic Energy Research Institute, *Forty Years' History of KAERI in Pictures* (Daejeon, 2000)].

power generation and research, and suggested the introduction of a new reactor of much smaller capacity for research only.[61]

The committee's final decision in April 1968 allowed the KECO to undertake the construction and operation of the first nuclear power plant; and then, the OAE would be in charge of security regulations, the development of reactor technologies, the management of new and used nuclear fuels, and the training of technical operators. Even the fact-oriented official history of the AERI could not conceal its bewilderment

61 Yook Jong-Chul, *"Hangukjeollyeok Jeollyeogeopche Machiya"* ["The Standpoint of the Korea Electric Company,"] *Dong-A Ilbo,* 17 Feburary. 1968.

by pointing out that the decision was apparently not drawn out of the meetings where the desirability of creating a new bureau was the main topic; and that debates or discussions over who should be in charge of the construction of the second, or the third nuclear power plants never took place, as the decision was confined to the first one.[62] To Park Ik-Su, the committee's decision was made not only against the original law (Atomic Energy Act) that mandated the OAE to take charge of all the national programs pertaining to atomic energy and their legislations and regulations, but it also bypassed the lawful process that required the Atomic Energy Committee to review important policy issues. Why such a sudden decision after a long pondering? Park strongly suspected that there was a collusive deal between the military government and the Korean representative agent for a reactor provider, as the Cheongwadae (the executive office of the President) was deeply involved in this nuclear power plant enterprise to the extent that it was rumored to be the "Cheongwadae project."[63] By contrast, Lee Chang-Geon was far more acquiescent about the government's explanation that the KECO had a definite advantage of being able to get a loan secured on landed property and the power plants it owned. Furthermore, he recalled that it was KECO's decision, not the committee's, to choose a pressurized water reactor manufactured by an American company, Westinghouse, which was one of the light water-cooled reactor types, over the gas-cooled reactor types that had been used in British and French nuclear power plants. It was partly because

62 Korea Atomic Energy Research Institute, *Hangugwonjaryeogyeonguso 30nyeonsa* , 134-135.

63 Park, "Atomic Energy and I," 371-375.

the U.S. Export-Important Bank could offer a better interest rate on the loan.[64] Although a detailed account of the KECO's takeover requires a thorough historical investigation, it is nevertheless clear that the military government was able to redefine the function of the nuclear bureaucracy without taking legislative procedures. Like in many other cases, the military government was above the law.

Conclusion

The three-body nuclear bureaucracy of the Office of Atomic Energy, the Atomic Energy Committee, and the Atomic Energy Research Institute built its reputation for an all-around science administration in the early 1960s. However, its influence on the most significant nuclear enterprise of all—the planning and managing of the construction of nuclear power plants—had since ebbed, and so did its bureaucratic standing. If 1968 was a turning point for nuclear bureaucracy as it ceded its major territory of commercial nuclear power to the electric utility company, 1973 was then the year that sealed its downward movement. The once cabinet-level status of the OAE (원자력원), which had already been downgraded one step to the vice-ministry level (원자력청), was re-designated to the Ministry of Science and Technology's Office of Atomic En-

64 Lee Chang-Geon, "Naui Wonjaryeok Hoego," 347-350. Lee Chang-Geon maintained that the Korea Electric Company's Chief Technology Officer, Kim Jong-Joo, who had received nuclear training in both the U.K. and the U.S., made a decision on the reactor type. Unlike Park Ik-Su, Lee was generally positive about the KECO's takeover, as he thought the company maintained a good working relationship with the OAE and the AREI for policy and technical advice.

ergy (원자력국) in a much smaller size. The statutory authority of the AEC became concurrently obscure, existing in little more than a mere name. Some measures were taken to strengthen the AERI's competitiveness. A new legislation made the AERI a government-funded yet private corporate entity, similar to the status of the Korea Institute of Science and Technology, changing its name into the Korea Atomic Energy Research Institute (KAERI) with the addition of the two previously detached organizations, the Radiation Institute and the Radiation Agricultural Institute. Director of the KAERI was then given more discretionary power in the personnel system, the creation and abolition of laboratories, and budget spending. These changes led to a notable increase in the number of employees (which more than doubled in seven years from 443 people in 1973, in contrast to a meager increase of 46 people in the previous seven years) and a longer tenure of directors (only four directors appointed between 1973 and 1990, in contrast to 13 directors between 1959 and 1973)[65]. Nevertheless, as long as the Korea Electric Company maintained the authority to plan, construct, and manage nuclear power plants, the KAERI's role was limited to that of a sidekick—providing technical know-hows and producing a cadre of research personnel to accomplish the goal of localization, or "Koreanization," of technologies for nuclear power plants and the fuels.[66] In the years to come, the relationship between the KAERI and the KECO evolved into one of rivals as well as of collaborators. This cooperative yet contentious relationship was a product of the military regime.

---

65 Korea Atomic Energy Research Institute, *Hangugwonjaryeogyeonguso 30nyeonsa, 145-147.*

66 For Koreanization, see Kim, *Wonjaryeokbidangil: Wonjeongisurui Guksanhwa.*

The technology gap was unquestionably a significant policy issue to underdeveloped countries like Korea, for there were many technologies to acquire and develop, and multiple ways to fill the gap. Relevant decisions had to be made. Early technocrats like Park Chul-Jae and Yoon Se-Won, who played pivotal roles in the formation of the nuclear bureaucracy, were convinced that the operation of a small reactor would afford practical knowledge and research experience much needed to build commercial nuclear power plants and expand the area of nuclear studies. They conceived the nuclear bureaucracy as an all-around science bureaucracy, at least for the time being, which would allow them to fill the knowledge gap as well as the technology gap. To this end, they asserted, scientists should be on top rather than on tap in a nuclear administration. By contrast, Park Ik-Su was a different kind of bureaucrat: a science-writer-turned-science-advisor. Although he was never engaged in day-to-day administration of the research program, Park Ik-Su assumed an influential position as a science advisor—a role much valued because he was neither a technocrat nor an insider. Park Ik-Su's view that science policy should be considered in conjunction with other national policies had a strong appeal to the military government gearing up for an all-out effort to achieve economic self-reliance. He rendered his talent and energy in the service of the military regime, and yet he was also concerned about its innate problems—collusion, corruption, and ignorance of lawful procedures—and he continuously opined this outlook through the press, even when his service was no longer called for. Park never accepted the proposition that might handcuff the nuclear bureaucracy in the power plant project by transferring its prerogatives to a utility company like the KECO. From 1968 on, however, the military government laid out a clear bureaucratic arrangement—the division of labor between the AERI and the KECO—for constructing commercial nuclear power plants with indigenous technology. This governmental drive resulted in a significant expansion of the KAERI, but its autonomy nonetheless suffered. Even the word "atomic" was stripped from its name, as it officially came to be called the Korea "Advanced" Energy Research Institute throughout the 1980s.

In the course of the bureaucratic changes in Korea's nuclear program, one can notice the invocation of nationalism at the individual as well as governmental levels. Although nationalism might have diverse meanings in the social and political settings of the post-Korean War decades, it is safe to say that many of the first-generation nuclear scientists worked with nationalist fervor. They were willing to sacrifice themselves—their academic careers and even their health (for potential exposure to radioactivity)—for participating in the nation-building process with their specialized knowledge. For this reason, nationalism was sometimes employed as an ideological weapon in the demarcation of the line between experts and laymen. Under the military government, science and technology became increasingly important as a central piece in the ideology of developmental nationalism. Therefore, Richard J. Samuels's technonationalism, the view of technology as the source of national security and economic prosperity in an integrated way, may as well be applied here. Yet technonationalism can still entail diverse implications at the individual level. It will be interesting to see how technonationalism united people to work together in the unprecedented administrative arrangement between a state-funded private research institute and a state-run private company—a bureaucratic setup that was uniquely Korean.

The "Koreanization" of Nuclear Power Technology*

The Case of a Joint Design

Byung-Koo Kim

The original concept of the Joint Design was a brainchild of Han Pil-soon (한필순), as crystallized in his inauguration speech as Korea Atomic Energy Research Institute (KAERI, 한국원자력연구소) president on April 9, 1984. He said, "The only way for a developing country to reach nuclear power technical self-reliance is to take part in the commercial Nuclear Power Plant (NPP) construction projects in the areas of KAERI's expertise. We have no money, no time, and no experienced manpower to bring it up from scratch." That was the beginning of a long road to bring KAERI to take responsibilities in the NPP reactor systems and initial core design technologies, which was assumed by taking a prime contractor's role in the Yeonggwang (영광) Nuclear (YGN) project.

The first Joint Design concept was put into practice in 1985, when

---

* This essay is an excerpt from Byung-Koo Kim's memoir, *Nuclear Silk Road: The "Koreanization" of Nuclear Power Technology* (Scotts Valley, CA, 2011).

the reload fuel localization of the Pressurized Water Reactor (PWR) project was started with Kraftwerk Union (KWU) of Germany. Already seventy-plus KAERI fuel engineers were sent to KWU fuel design center in Erlangen, Germany, to conduct the core analysis of reload together with the German counterparts in a joint design under a technology transfer contract. All design tools were transferred to KAERI before the engineers returned to Korea by 1987.The first reload core fuels designed by KWU and KAERI, then manufactured by Korea Nuclear fuel Company (KNFC, 한국원자력연료 주식회사) in Daedeok (대덕), were being loaded into Kori (고리) units. This successful experience of Joint Design in the reload fuel projects gave a strong impetus for a bigger and more complicated Nuclear Steam Supply System (NSSS) reactor systems design project to be conducted in a similar fashion. Now the stage was set to expand the fuel experience to the entire NPP reactor systems with different actors.

Preparation

Immediately after Combustion Engineering (CE) was selected as the successful bidder of the YGN and NSSS partner company in September of 1986, the Power Reactor Systems Division at KAERI was realigned to be the same as the CE Windsor organization. We knew right away the most efficient way to absorb the system design technology would be to emulate the mentor-to-be's technical infrastructure as much as possible to prepare for the upcoming Joint Design missions on a one-to-one approach in five technical disciplines: reactor engineering (RE), fluid systems engineering (FSE), mechanical design and analysis (MDA), instrument and control (I&C), and safety analysis (SA). The manpower pool within KAERI had reached over eighty when the very first team of forty-six (Group A) was sent to Windsor at the end of 1986, having grown from thirty-three members just about a year before. Already word had gotten around in and out of KAERI that the most ambitious nuclear project in history was about to begin. We were assured and thus fortunate to be able to hire new recruits outside of the government manpower authorization limits, since the entire manpower cost was to be supported by the Yeonggwang project cost once the contracts were signed. The new Power Reactor System Division at KAERI (PRSD) team was composed of five technical groups of highly educated engineers with graduate degrees (about 50 percent with MSs, 30 percent with PhDs, and 20 percent with BSs) in engineering disciplines, mainly nuclear, mechanical, electrical, chemical, and physics backgrounds.

Conversational English training courses were held at KAERI with native US speakers. With all their academic credentials, the KAERI team may have appeared to be well- or even over-qualified; however, we had a definite shortage of (in fact, zero) experienced manpower with NPP systems design backgrounds. No one with such qualifications existed in Korea as of 1986. We were all young, well educated, and well motivated, but had no practical experiences to speak of. The only way to overcome this shortage was to put the team through a series of rigorous training courses in combinations of Class-Room Training (CRT), On-the-job Training (OJT), and On-the-job Participation (OJP), later called "Joint Design" or "Joint System Design," plus field trips to NPPs and component manufacturing sites.

One crucial six-week Class Room Training (CRT) course was organized by the IAEA Technical Cooperation project specially tailored for the KAERI system design engineers at the KAERI campus in October 1986. A brief Memorandum of Understanding for the system design advanced training was signed between CE and KAERI only two weeks after the successful bidder announcement. Everyone was eager and willing to take the risk, to get on with the training even though the main contract negotiations had yet to start. We were able to bring in most of the CE engineering managers or supervisors as the lecturers. CE management put high priority in sending their best technical managers, all of them for the first time, to Korea. Regis Matzie (reactor engineering), Dan Peck (mechanical design and analysis), and Bill Gill (instrument and control) were among the first group of CE managers who came to Korea. During and after the formal CRT hours, they were enthusiastic about the first opportunity to get to know each of their Korean counterparts besides delivering the technical materials. Matzie recalls his first visit to KAERI:

> I was surprised to meet so many young PhDs, but Kuh Jung-Eui (구정의) and his team made me feel right at home from the very first day. We went out for dinner with the whole RE group, got to know them personally, and I was impressed with their engineering enthusiasm. I felt they had the right DNA in mental capacity to master the system design know-how's in no time. Kuh's team appeared more academic than practical, but it suited fine with my area of reactor engineering."[1]

1 Author's interview with Regis Matzie at Windsor. Octorber 2010.

Obviously, this kind of initial building of rapport had lasting effects as they moved to Windsor for the Joint Design in the coming months. Mental comradeship was forming between mentors and mentees among engineers, supervisors, and managers from both sides, overcoming the cultural and geographical barriers. Perhaps the degree of camaraderie between two organizations would differ from team to team depending on the personal character of each of the managers, but I overall felt comfortable enough to judge that we were in for a long haul and had the right teachers and right mentors from the very beginning.

We took the CE lecturers to Gyeongju (경주), the ancient capital of the Shilla (신라) dynasty, after the first CRT (Class Room Training), which turned out to be effective in understanding Korean culture and nurturing the team-building. (They saw the original Cheonmachong (천마총) and Shilla golden crown at the Gyeongju National Museum then.) As a symbol of lasting cooperation and friendship, KAERI presented the replica of the Shilla golden crown to CE in 1988 (fortunately, this one symbolic piece still proudly occupies the main entrance hall of the Westinghouse Windsor plant today). This small gesture of cooperation made over two decades ago is worth revisiting today. It exemplifies how the original dream of technical self-reliance on the Korean side became a reality with CE as the strong partner and mentor, as engraved on a small plaque attached to the crown, reading:

> This exact replica of the ancient Shilla Gold Crown (Cheonmachong, circa 5th century A.D.) is presented to Combustion Engineering, Inc. on the occasion of the KAERI Windsor Site Office opening ceremony held on the twenty-ninth of January 1988. This symbolizes long lasting partnership between CE and KAERI through this Joint Design and

Technology Transfer during the implementation of Yeonggwang 3 & 4 Project. CE's contribution in helping to establish indigenous nuclear power technologies is recognized for the energy independence in the Republic of Korea.

Technology Transfer, Korean Style

It took a relatively short time before the "Korean Pilgrims" started to be integrated into the CE Windsor NSSS engineering departments. After a brief two-week orientation of CRT, given to the newly arrived Korean engineers (Group A) to Windsor in January 1987, each one was assigned to his respective NSSS engineering department for the following four months of OJT. This was the crucial period for the KAERI team to prove themselves worthy of conducting the NSSS system design activities for the first time, while fully being integrated into the existing CE infrastructure.

At the end of the four-month OJT program, every Korean engineer was evaluated and declared fit for service without a single failure. Despite the English language deficiencies, every team member survived the initial tests of functioning as a design engineer to initiate, to review, and to obtain supervisors' approval on a mock-up design activity. The first informal progress report from Lee Byung-Ryung (이병령) or 'BR Lee,' the first engineering manager of the KAERI team at Windsor) was sent to President Han via a seventeen pages of hand-written facsimile message at the end of March 1987.

Lee was expressing his satisfaction on the progress of the OJT of each team member in preparation for the real Joint Design to start as soon as the formal Yeonggwang contract was signed. Detailed curriculum of subtasks, objective, design description, output products, interface requirements, and schedule of design activities for each member were being implemented as agreed. CE supervisors were evaluating KAERI members' knowledge on the technical subject matter as well as communication skills. Lee's overall conclusion in the fax report was confidence in the system design technical areas per se; however, he made a recommendation to improve the project management capabilities in planning, scheduling, manpower loading, interface coordination, and, most of all, quality control and quality assurance. These were the areas the KAERI management was not well prepared for at the beginning. In fact, we did not know what it would take to integrate vast system design activities across different disciplines in reaching the major milestones in the project.

Lee's recommendation was well taken once the contract was duly signed and the full scope Joint System Design activities commenced in May 1987. Thanks to the hard work of several industry-minded KAERI project management teams at Windsor, the need to establish an Engineering Logic Network was recognized by the KAERI management. They were able to acquire sufficient know-how from CE internal practices on how best to set up the KAERI specific system design integration processes, coupled with the schedule and cost control. A separate KAERI Windsor Site Office was created with the special mission to build up the project management capacities, including schedule control, quality control, and document control. Lee made an important contribution during the initial period of KAERI's settlement into the bona fide system design engineer's role at Windsor. All members were asked to come into work thirty minutes earlier and stay two hours after the normal working hours, even on Saturdays, for internal seminars. No one dared to complain as there was so much to learn and absorb. Lee provided leadership to promote useful means to better organize one's work activities, to learn about other members' work activities, as well as to improve English communication skills, including how to raise questions to CE mentors. In hindsight, his major role as the KAERI engineering manager in Windsor at the early stage is to be recognized in building team spirit. In the 1990s, Lee made one more major contribution to the Korean nuclear scene while serving as the project manager for the Uljin (울진) 3&4 system design at KAERI, in selecting the Korean Standard Nuclear Power Plant (KSNP) model for the Korean Peninsula Energy Development Organization (KEDO, 한반도 에너지 개발 기구) project with Uljin 3&4 as the reference plant. (This topic is covered in Chapter 7 of Kim's forthcoming memoir.) Lee also served as the Yuseong (유성) District Office superintendent, an elected public official post in Daejeon (대전) city, administering for Daedeok Science Town (대덕 연구 단지) in the 2000s.

Additional waves of KAERI design engineers arrived in Windsor in 1987 and 1988 in Group B (thirteen) and Group C (twenty-two) to join the Joint System Design activities following the similar CRT and OJT training as Group A. Altogether, over two hundred KAERI engineers were dispatched during the project life cycle, which peaked to one hundred and twenty in 1988, accumulating over three hundred man-years of expatriate experience at Windsor. Beginning in 1989, KAERI manpower receded gradually as they completed the Joint Design assignments and returned home (the Initial Core Design team was the first to return) to build on the project design center at Daedeok. [2]

Integration with the Mentor

Designing and building a nuclear power plant is a complex task involving thousands of highly trained, dedicated professionals in several dozen different organizations, mostly made up of engineers in many disciplines. Among the most difficult, thus challenging, task would be the system design of the reactor system, or in the industry jargon, the Nuclear Steam Supply System ('N triple S'). An added dimension to an already complex task on our hands was to integrate organizations from two countries from opposite sides of the Pacific, to start the design process in the US first and then to move the entire design center to Korea to complete the second half under the so-called "Transition Plan."

Reactor system design activities are categorized in three different levels. Level 1 design is the "conceptual design," involving several hundred independent activities to identify the skeleton of the reactor system for the intended power level, the process system, and the safety system. Level 2 design involves roughly eighteen hundred separate design activities, called "basic design," enough to issue the Preliminary Safety Analysis Report (PSAR) and design specifications for the long-lead items such as the reactor vessel and steam generators. Level 3, called "detail design," typically involves twenty thousand design activities to generate all the

2 Lee Ik-hwan, Annual Report of Windsor Site Office, KAERI/GP-62-76/89, Internal Report, December 1990.

documents and drawings for construction, procurements, and final commissioning start-up tests. When a utility orders a new NPP, typically the reactor vendor has a certified basic design from the national regulatory authority, and the detail design has to be redone from the reference plant design to suit the specific site and upgrade items as necessary.

Difficulty in the job assignments for KAERI members arose during the first year of Joint System Design at Windsor in 1987. It had to occur as both parties were bound to have conflicting views. KAERI's team was determined to learn the core technology in the shortest time possible while stationed at Windsor (each one was given a two-year term) so they wanted to get to the most challenging design activities as possible. In addition, KAERI was in the customer's position to CE, although they shared a mentor/mentee relationship. We made sure in the Joint System Design contract that KAERI would provide 50 percent of the overall design activities in volume without knowing exactly which 50 percent would be its share.

On the other hand, CE was given the overall responsibility and contractual warranty obligations should they fail to meet the delivery deadlines or performance warranty. Each of KAERI member's capabilities and communication skills was still not fully proven for CE to be comfortable, although they all had passed the minimum qualification test after the initial four months OJT at Windsor. This mutually uncomfortable situation was more acute in the fluid systems engineering than others, mainly because of the nature of design activities being more repetitive and less innovative, and perhaps due to the personalities involved. It could be boring work for someone with a PhD degree and at a relative young age. In the area of instrumentation and control, oftentimes the design activities crossed boundaries between the system design and component design due to its very nature, thereby adding to the complexity. (Although BR Lee, the engineering manager, had some problems with job assignments, he was up against some tough-minded CE managers and had to make stands that were not always popular. All in all, he did a good job in a situation that was unprecedented.) As the years passed by, however, these initial problems did get resolved satisfactorily for both sides. I could confirm the facts through numerous interviews with many from both sides during the writing of this book. Of course, the final outcome of the technology transfer without a single drop-out among over two hundred KAERI expatriate engineers speaks for itself.[3]

Invariably the system design activities involved producing documents, be it design specifications and design data for procurement or manufacturing, or interface documents to other entities like the architect engineers, or calculation sheets and drawings. Almost all of these documents are considered company proprietary and become part of the company's intellectual property. Each document is approved and signed off by the writer (cognizant engineer), an independent reviewer, and an approval authority from the technical supervisors. The integrated team of the Joint System Design members learned to produce literally thousands of these documents in a highly professional manner. The system of document control, known as the Nuclear Engineering Documentation System (NEDS), originated by CE during the previous Palo Verde project, was employed. This document control system added order to the management of these documents and proved quite beneficial to all parties during

3 Author's interview with Jim Veirs at Windsor. Octorber 2010.

the course of the project. The system allowed virtually free access to all technical proprietary documents to Koreans at any time. The document control system was indicative of CE's open and transparent corporate mentality.

This corporate attitude was the main difference from its competitor when we selected CE over Westinghouse in the first place, and was found to be faithfully practiced during the course of the project. I could safely say that CE's attitude was to give Koreans everything they had, every 'know-how' they knew, without any reservations. At one time in the early period, CE Windsor had their internal discussion on the subject of as to what level CE's proprietary technology should be open to the Koreans. Vice President Bob Newman made this point clear to everyone:

> Remember, this opportunity is once in our lifetime. If we don't succeed in transferring all we can to the Koreans, then our technology would be of no use anymore, and we might as well throw it into the Connecticut River.[4]

This one simple anecdote represented the entire corporate culture of CE on the technology transfer. It was a true blessing for Korea in reaching its goal of self-reliance. KAERI was able to establish its own document control system administered by the Design Document Control Center (DDCC) at Daedeok with a fully functioning electronic database accessible from any authorized desk-top PC in the intranet.

---

4 Author's interview with Jim Veirs at Windsor. Octorber 2010.

Transition Plan

The original plan to relocate the system design center physically from CE to KAERI was imbedded in the Joint System Design and the Technology Transfer contract documents, stipulating that we shall reach a concrete transition plan within eighteen months after the contract. It was one of the most important tasks given to me as the project manager of the YGN System Design to reach a mutually agreeable plan with my counterpart, James Crawford, director of NSSS Engineering at CE. After many meetings and deliberations, we were able to sign a document called the "Transition Plan" on May 1, 1988. It was to implement the physical relocation of manpower and design tools, including computer codes, design documents, and supporting infrastructures. Within a year's time, the Yeonggwang reactor system design center would be fully operational at KAERI's Daedeok campus without interrupting the overall project schedule. This plan would also involve relocation of CE supervisory personnel to live in Daejeon for a longer period (a total of fifty man-years of CE supervisory staff was allocated for Daedeok assignments) with their families, plus gradual return of all KAERI expatriate engineers back to their home base. It was an ambitious plan to achieve. The overall project milestone of PSAR submittal to the Korean regulatory body and serious licensing discussions were beginning in mid-1988. Heavy components like the reactor vessel and steam generators were being casted and forged at the Korea Heavy Industries Corporation (KHIC, 한국중공업) Changwon (창원) plant based on our system design specifications, and the construction activities were moving into high gear by Hyundai Construction Company (현대건설) at the Yeonggwang site. There was no question in anyone's mind that the center of gravity for the project was moving to Korea. We had to hurry back to be closer to the real actions as a consequence of the system design output.

The first CE technical staff who came to Daejeon for an extended period was Robert Kirkman from Windsor in January 1988 to install and verify the computer codes at the KAERI computer center. His job was to hand-carry the source codes together with the binary codes for the system design. Over one hundred and ten codes (CE-owned codes, third-party-owned codes, plus some commercial codes) were installed at KAERI, followed by thorough verification checks.

By mid-1988, all design codes were running flawlessly in time for the KAERI design team's return home. Together with the documents that had already been delivered to KAERI beginning in 1987, the Design Center was well prepared to support the continuation of the system design in Daejeon. Over the course of the project, forty-six hundred proprietary documents and drawings were physically relocated to or developed by the Design Document Control Center.

Kirkman returned back to Windsor after a six-month stay in Daejeon. His working and living experience in Korea alleviated much worry from many CE staff who had some apprehension of coming to live in Korea according to the Transition Plan. In fact, his first hand working and living experience as a first-timer in a strange foreign country with a totally different culture turned out to be quite positive. His experience demonstrated to CE that comfortable living accommodations were readily available in a welcoming Korean community where local people were anxious to assist in any way. Undoubtedly it was more of a culture shock for CE staff to live in Daejeon than for KAERI staff to live in Windsor since no CE engineers spoke Korean, while the KAERI engineers were reasonably proficient in English.

The initial batch of KAERI engineers began returning home by the end of 1988. On April 18, 1989, CE Daedeok Office was formally opened with Jack Pucak as its first site manager. Pucak's role was mainly to liaise design activities between Windsor and Daedeok. Tom Natan, the engineering manager for the YGN, and Dan Peck, manager of mechanical design and analysis, came to stay three to four months in Daedeok to expedite the in-situ decision-making.

With more than two years of Joint System Design experiences at Windsor and the gradual return of experienced design engineers to Korea, and with the design infrastructures being ready with codes and documents in full operational mode, we felt reasonably comfortable to move the design center to Daedeok in 1989. Integration of the system design support team at Daedeok with the newly returning KAERI engineers from Windsor posed less of a problem than expected, as a continuous inflow and outflow program to and from Windsor was in place. Every move was in line with the Transition Plan. The first major task at the new design center was to finalize the Final Safety Analysis Report (FSAR) reflecting all the design upgrades and specifics as the plant was being built. Over eleven hundred design activities were scheduled to be performed at Daedeok, with KAERI engineers in the lead and CE supervisory functions as needed. Start-up test guidelines and regulatory updates were among the highest-priority items. A real motivation for the system engineers was the opportunity to eye-witness the manufacturing and construction of the components and systems they designed for verification and trouble-shooting any anomalies with implementing the design. Frequent visits to the KHIC Changwon plant, where the major components like the reactor vessels and steam generators were being fabricated, and to the construction site at Yeonggwang became a routine part of the design verification activities. KAERI Yeonggwang Site Office was formally opened in 1992 to expedite the start-up support activities.

Warranty Conditions

The YGN contract was indeed one-of-a-kind in many respects, requiring the foreign subcontractors like CE and S&L to take full warranty responsibilities while being the subcontractors to the Korean prime contractors: KHIC, KAERI, Korea Power Engineering Company (KOPEC, 한국전력주식회사), and KNFC. Since the Korean prime contractors had no proven past credentials of delivering the whole NPP at that time, Korea Electric Power Corporation (KEPCO, 한국전력공사) had to make a special provision to induce CE and S&L to assume the warranty responsibilities by making the sub-contracts into tripartite agreements including the KEPCO signature. This measure was intended to provide additional protection in case the prime contractors failed to deliver on their roles and responsibilities. However, as it turned out, this additional protection was not necessary as the Korean prime contractors all managed to meet their obligations. CE had to take the largest share of warranty obligations as the NSSS technology holder. The scope of their warranties included:

- The thermal output performance at the steam generator outlet
- Delivery schedule

- System design accuracy
- Interface data correctness
- Regulatory licensing (from the Korean authority)
- The fuel cycle costs

It was clear from the beginning that the technology holder, CE, was the only qualified entity to assume the above warrantee conditions. These conditions included clear formulas for assessing the financial penalties in case any of the warrantees were not met. The most important of them all was the thermal output performance warranty. This warranty included a financial penalty that could accrue in the millions of dollars should the thermal output be less than the warranted designed value. It was a measure of the success of the project that the Yeonggwang Project demonstrated all warranted conditions, and there were no contractual claims against any of the parties following start-up and full power demonstration testing. The plant was unconditionally accepted for commercial operation by KEPCO on March 30, 1995.

The true sign of technical self-reliance must come with the ability to take up the full warranty conditions, including the financial burden. The Korean local prime contractors (which were identical to the YGN case) had to wait for the second NPP project, Uljin 3&4 signed in 1991, to assume all the warranty obligations for the first time. This was the main reason Uljin 3&4 NPPs were the first KSNP units to be called "Korean Standardized Nuclear Plant" (KSNP).

Manpower Build-up

One may recall the original system design technical staff was only thirty-three when the Power Reactor Systems Design division was initiated at KAERI in 1985. In the next ten years' time, these core members witnessed a dramatic growth to about four hundred technical staff responsible for the reactor system design of multiple NPP construction projects ongoing simultaneously: YGN, Uljin 3&4, Yeonggwang 5&6, KEDO project for North Korea, and Uljin 5&6. By the 1995 timeframe, the entire KAERI project operation was at its peak with five project divisions (Yeonggwang, Uljin, Wolseong (월성), Light Power Reactor (LWR) fuel, and KEDO) supported by the Design Division in matrix organization. As the NPP projects had about a two-year time interval between new projects, a continuous flux of manpower from one project to another, and from design division to project division (or vice versa), was necessary to maintain the proper level of manpower loading for each project at any given time. A project management team was dedicated to each project for interface control, schedule, cost, and quality control, in addition to managing the site offices away from the Daedeok head office (Windsor, Yeonggwang, Uljin, and Wolseong construction sites).

The system design technology was central to and rested in the Design Division composed of five technical departments: Reactor Engineering, Fluid Systems Engineering, Mechanical Design, Instrumentation & Control, and Safety Analysis. The YGN occupied the largest manpower share (nine hundred and eighty-eight man-years, at least) to cope with the technology transfer simultaneously with the joint system design, which started at Windsor first then transferred to Daedeok in the middle of the project. While the Joint System Design (JSD) manpower was implementing the design activities according to the project construction schedule, additional System Design Support manpower was allocated to follow the technology transfer in digesting technical know-how.

CE mobilized about three hundred man-years of effort for the first project, which dropped to minimal after several repeat projects. More JSD manpower was needed at Daedeok after the Transition Plan. About half of the overall manpower was dedicated to the SD Support activities at Daedeok to conduct activities including:

- Mock-up design and repeat design on technically significant activities
- Technical review and analysis reports on selected proprietary documents
- Preparation of the internal standard design manuals and procedures
- Establishing the design Quality Assurance system to acquire the ASME N-stamp certificate
- Install, verify and maintain all design computer codes imported from CE to be fully operational at all times
- Operate the Design Document Control Center (DDCC) at Daedeok to sort, store, and distribute.

This extra effort was the reserve manpower trained for the coming new projects like Uljin 3&4 and Yeonggwang 5&6. In fact, what may appear to be excessive manpower loading at the beginning, turned out to be the exemplary program of manpower training and build-up to start from CRT to OJT to JSD for the very first project YGN, then moving on to subsequent projects. This was all possible due to the fact that Korea kept on building the standardized fleet of twelve more NPPs during the last twenty years: Yeonggwang 3&4, Uljin 3&4, Yeonggwang 5&6, Uljin 5&6, Sin-Kori (신고리) 1&2, Sin-Wolseong (신월성) 1&2, all of the same design Generation II NPPs (the suffix "Shin" means "new" in Korean, thus "Sin-Kori" refers to the new NPP site adjacent to the "old Kori" site). The ultimate sign of technical self-reliance comes from the ability to take up the warranty responsibilities for the performance and delivery of the new NPP. While CE was responsible for the warranties for the YGN, KAERI (later KOPEC) was responsible for all subsequent system design projects from Uljin 3&4.

Mission "95-by-95"

On December 7, 1995, a quiet celebration was going on at the KEPCO head office in Seoul following the technical self-reliance evaluation symposium. It was declared by internal as well as external experts that the dual project milestones of Yeonggwang Unit 3 going into commercial operation and the technical self-reliance goal of 95 percent had indeed been reached. The component design and equipment supply of the reactor coolant pump, man-machine interface system in the main control room, and the third-party-owned computer codes were the only remaining 5 percent yet to be localized. The unique strategy of the joint design seemed to have worked to overcome the shortages of experienced manpower, budget, and time. We all experienced a big sigh of relief that the major milestone was achieved. At least we knew we could replicate the design of the same NPPs indigenously. The next challenge was how to move up to a truly Korean reactor model design to compete with the Generation III models being developed by other international suppliers. Every indication was positive in that we were ready to take up the next challenge: the Korean Next Generation Reactor (KNGR) development.

From the day one of the very beginning of the YGN project, KEPCO announced the goal of reaching 95 percent of technical self-reliance for the entire NPP plant design and construction by the year 1995, when the Unit 3 was to be completed, thus the nickname "95-by-95." It was not clear at all at the beginning what was meant by "95 percent self-reliance" and how to measure its progress. Thanks to KEPCO's rigorous system of accountability in project management, the project management team from Electric Power Group Cooperation Council (EPGCC) was able to agree on the formula with relative weighing factors that could result in an evaluation of the 95 percent goal by the year 1995.

It is interesting to note that the fuel design/manufacturing, and site construction technologies were deemed 100 percent self-reliant by 1995 due to their past experiences in the existing NPP construction and reload fuel projects. Relative weighing factors were agreed upon primarily based on the contract prices covering the entire spectrum of nuclear power technologies in design, manufacturing, and construction. Each nuclear entity (which formed the Electric Power Group Cooperation Council from 1985 on) knew for sure that they were in for the most challenging episode in the company's history, as each one was assured of exclusive rights and responsibilities in the standardized fleet of NPPs to come.

One of my prime responsibilities as the project manager of system design was to set the annual detail implementation plans for technical self-reliance and confirm it for the monthly progress checks. Numerous internal and external meetings were held at Daedeok, Changwon (창원), and Seoul to discuss, modify, and argue with other entities. It seemed like a nightmare scenario in those days to trace thousand of different design activities and the status of where we lacked confidence. In hindsight, it was the necessary step in gaining confidence, and, most of all, beginning to comprehend the scope of our shortcomings, that is, what we really did not know. There was the natural process of gaining the "know-why" beyond the "know-how" by repeating the nearly identical NPP construction projects and having to defend the adequacy of the design to Korea Institute of Nuclear Safety (KINS, 한국원자력안전기술원) and KEPCO for each new project to reconfirm the application of the previous project design and to justify the changes that were incorporated into the new projects.

In parallel, the Technology Transfer contract was implemented to 1) transfer documents, codes, patent rights, 2) conduct a series of training courses for the system designers, 3) separate training for the supervisory capacity and project management, 4) procure special computer control equipment. Additional efforts were made on the System 80+ R&D projects together with CE to enhance further understanding of the know-whys leading to the next-generation power reactors to come. In that sense, the mission "95-by-95" was accomplished over and beyond the original expectations. There was a good reason to celebrate on that night of December 7, 1995.[5]

5 Han Ki-in, Yeonggwang 3,4Hogi Wonjarogyetongsaeop Choejongbogoseo: Wonjarogyetongseolgye Gisuljarip Chujin GyeongheomjipYeonggwang 3&4 Final Report on the Reactor System Design Project: Technical Self-reliance Experiences, KAERI, December. 31, 1995.

Index

P

R

S

T

U

W

Y

About Authors

Youngsoo Bae, Professor of History and currently Dean of the College of Humanities, Seoul National University, is interested in American social history. His books include *Labor in Retreat: Class and Community Among Men's Clothing Workers of Chicago, 1871-1929* (SUNY Press 2001) and *In Search of an Alternative to American Exceptionalism* (2011), which is written in Korean. His current research interests focus on the development of American civilization in the global context.

Buhm Soon Park is Associate Professor and Head of the Graduate School of Science and Technology Policy at Korea Advanced Institute of Science and Technology (KAIST). He received his Ph.D. in history of science from the Johns Hopkins University in 1999, and subsequently worked as a historian of biomedical sciences and research policy at the U.S. National Institutes of Health (NIH) before coming to KAIST in 2007. Professor Park specializes in the history of twentieth-century science and the development of science and technology policy. He is currently writing a book on the relationship between bureaucratic autonomy and science policy, examining the rise of the NIH as the major patron of American biomedicine.

Byung-Koo Kim is the Senior Research Fellow at Khalifa University's Nuclear Engineering Department in Abu Dhabi since 2011. Previously, he served seven years as a Director of Technical Cooperation at the International Atomic Energy Agency (IAEA) in Vienna, assisting many developing countries to establish nuclear infrastructures for peaceful uses of nuclear energy. A Ph.D. in applied mechanics from California Institute of Technology, Dr. Kim worked for the Korea Atomic Energy Research Institute (KAERI) in Korea for 30 years. His recent memoir, *Nuclear Silk Road – The "Koreanization" of Nuclear Power Technology*, is based on his experience as a researcher at KAERI.

Manyong Moon is Research Professor at the Institute for the History of Science, Technology and Civilization, KAIST. He received his Ph.D. in the Interdisciplinary Program of History and Philosophy of Science at Seoul National University. His research area is in the history of science in Modern Korea, especially history of biology and agriculture and science and technology policies in Korea. His books include *The Formation of Modern Research System in Korea* (2010), and *A Documentary History of the Development of Modern Science in Korea* (2004), both written in Korean.

Morris Low is Associate Professor of Japanese History in the School of History, Philosophy, Religion and Classics at the University of Queensland. His recent books include: *East Asia Beyond the History Wars: Confronting the Ghosts of Violence* (co-authored) (Routledge, 2013); *Urban Modernity: Cultural Innovation in the Second Industrial Revolution* (co-authored) (MIT Press 2010); *Japan on Display: Photography and the Emperor* (Routledge 2006) and *Science and the Building of a New Japan* (Palgrave Macmillan 2005). He is an Adjunct Associate Professor at John Hopkins University and has held academic positions at Monash University and the

Australian National University.

Sulfikar Amir is Assistant Professor in the Division of Sociology, Nanyang Technological University, Singapore. His research interests are in science and technology studies, globalization, development, and risk and resilience. He is the author of *The Technological State in Indonesia: the Co-constitution of High Technology and Authoritarian Politics* (Routledge 2012).

Sungsoo Song is Associate Professor in the Department of Physics Education at Pusan National University in Korea. He received his Ph.D. in the Interdisciplinary Program of History and Philosophy of Science at Seoul National University in 2002. His major publications include *Moving the World without a Voice, Steel* (2004), *When Science and Technology Meet Culture* (2009), *Searching for the Interfaces between Science, Technology, and Society* (2011), all written in Korean.

Tae Gyun Park is Associate Professor at the Graduate School of International Studies, Seoul National University, where he received his Ph.D. in Korean History in 2000. His major publications include *Ally and Empire, Two Myths in the Korea-U.S. Relationship* (2006), which is written in Korean, and "Beyond the Myth: Reassessing the Security Crisis on the Korean Peninsula during the Mid-1960s" (2009).